Word for Windows

Quick & Easy

A Visual Approach for the Beginner

Welcome to **Quick & Easy.** Designed for the true novice, this new series covers basic tasks in a simple, learn-by-doing fashion. If that sounds like old news to you, take a closer look.

Quick & Easy books are a bit like picture books. They're for people who would rather see and do than read and ponder. The books are colorful. They're full of illustrations, and accompanying text that is straightforward, concise, and easy to read.

But don't waste your time reading about our **Quick & Easy** books; start learning your new software package instead. This **Quick & Easy** book is just the place to start.

Word for Windows™
Quick&*Easy*

Christian Crumlish

SYBEX®

San Francisco • Paris • Düsseldorf • Soest

Acquisitions Editor: Dianne King
Series Editor: Christian T. S. Crumlish
Editor: Richard Mills
Technical Editor: Cheryl Thoen
Word Processors: Ann Dunn and Susan Trybull
Series Designers: Helen Bruno and Ingrid Owen
Typesetter: Deborah Maizels
Production Coordinator: Catherine Mahoney
Indexer: Nancy Anderman Guenther
Cover Designer: Archer Design
Cover Illustrator: Richard Miller

Library of Congress Card Number: 92-61131
ISBN: 0-7821-1125-4

Manufactured in the United States of America
10 9 8 7 6 5 4 3 2 1

To Briggs,
who didn't want to see her name in print

ACKNOWLEDGMENTS

●

I'd like to thank Dianne King and David Clark, who encouraged me to propose this book. Thanks to Roger Gershon, Ingrid Owen, and Jennifer Booth for their part in planning and focusing the Quick & Easy concept.

My greatest thanks go to Richard Mills, who is everything an author could hope for in an editor—someone who understands what you're trying to say and helps you articulate it.

Helen Bruno, the series designer, did an incredible job balancing conflicting demands under nearly impossible conditions. She's responsible for the wonderful design of this book.

My thanks to technical editor Cheryl Thoen, word processors Ann Dunn and Susan Trybull, typesetter Deborah Maizels, production coordinator Catherine Mahoney, and indexer Nancy Guenther, all of whom performed above and beyond the call of duty when a mutiny would have been justified.

My mother and father, my brothers, and especially my sister, Jennifer, provided steady encouragement and support throughout the arduous writing process.

This book would not have been possible without the work of Charles Babbage, Ada Lovelace, and Alan Turing.

Thanks to the Geebers.

And thank you, Briggs Nisbet, for not killing me even as this book ate up larger and larger bites of our life together.

Contents
at a Glance

●

Contents

INTRODUCTION

●

Just because you work with a computer doesn't mean you like it. Most people find computers intimidating. Sure, they're supposed to make life easier. Then again, they were also supposed to make paper obsolete. (Right.) Often, a computer is just a nuisance—something else you've got to learn how to use. But it doesn't have to be that way.

Computers *are* getting easier to use, believe it or not. With Windows on your PC, you can get things done without having to know strange codes and commands, or even what's really going on inside the machine. Word for Windows is a very powerful, flexible word-processing program, but in some ways it's *too* powerful. There are so many options, so many doodads on the screen, so many choices, it can be bewildering. It's not your fault if you feel confused. I'm sure it's wonderful that someone can now put a picture inside a list inside a footnote, but are *you* ever going to do that?

This book will get you started with Word for Windows version 2.0 right away. I'll tell you just the things you'll need to know and steer you away from the stuff that would bog you down. You'll see how easy using a computer can be. The lessons in this book are bite-sized and easy to follow. They show you exactly what you should expect to see on the screen and tell you exactly what to do. You don't have to know anything about computers, DOS, Windows, word processing, or Word (you don't even have to know what all those things are).

What Makes It Quick and Easy?

As you can see, this book is short, under two hundred pages. The lessons are rarely longer than ten pages each. Best of all, I've eliminated all the junk you don't need to know, and believe me, you could fill a thousand-page book with the things you'll *never* use in Word. I'll always tell you the best and easiest ways to accomplish essential tasks. You'll be through this book in no time, and, in fact, after the first few lessons you'll know most of the important things about how to create documents in Word.

If you flip through this book, you'll see that there are tons of illustrations. I want you to feel confident at all times that you're on the right track and things are working the way they're supposed to. Anytime I describe something you should see on the screen or tell you to do something, I'll show you what it should look like. You can learn almost everything just by looking at the pictures! You'll also notice labels explaining items on the screen and occasional notes with helpful hints or explanations. Mainly, though, you'll learn by doing, following my step-by-step instructions.

At the beginning of each lesson is a suggested time to give you an idea of how long that lesson will take. It may go faster for you, or you may want to take more time. That's okay. Nobody's holding a stopwatch.

I Won't Steer You Wrong

This book will work best for you if you follow the instructions exactly and do the lessons in order. Although it is possible to learn from the lessons without following them exactly, you'll lose some of the reassurance you get from seeing exactly the same thing on your screen as you see in the illustration on the page.

There are variations from one computer to the next, from one screen to the next, from one printer to the next. Also, if you're not the first person to use your copy of Word, the previous users may have altered the setup in ways that may make your results differ slightly from the illustrations. If the differences are minor, you might as well just ignore them. If things look seriously different, you should have someone look at your setup and possibly return it to its beginning state.

Once you start a lesson, you'll be best off if you don't make idle changes. If you do, it may be hard to get things back the way they were. If you do something wrong by mistake, you can often get out of the situation by pressing Esc (the upper-leftmost key on most keyboards).

Help on the Way

If you are ever really stuck or if you wind up with strange problems not discussed in this book, keep in mind that Word has a very good Help feature. Use the Help Index command on the Help menu when you need information. You can then click a button labeled **Instructions** to get an explanation of how to use Help.

Using Your Mouse with Windows

This book assumes you are using a mouse. If you don't have one, you can still follow most of the instructions, but I highly recommend you get one. Windows was designed to be used with a mouse. Here are several mouse techniques you need to understand:

To *click* something, position the mouse pointer over that thing and then quickly press and release the left mouse button. For example, if I tell you to click the leftmost button on the Toolbar, what you do will look like this:

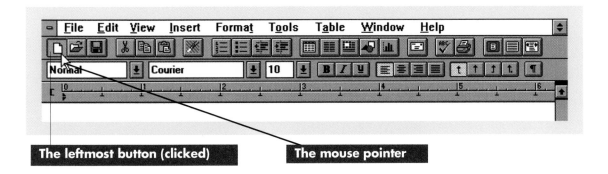

The leftmost button (clicked)   **The mouse pointer**

To *double-click* something, position the mouse pointer over that thing and then quickly press and release the left mouse button twice in a row.

To *drag* something, position the mouse pointer over it, press the left mouse button, and then *before releasing the mouse button* move the mouse so that the thing you clicked is visibly dragged across the screen.

To *pull down* a menu and select an option on it, position the mouse pointer over a menu name in the menu bar, press the left mouse button, and then drag the mouse toward you. When the specified option on the menu is highlighted, release the mouse button. For example, if I tell you to pull down the File menu and select New, what you do will look like this:

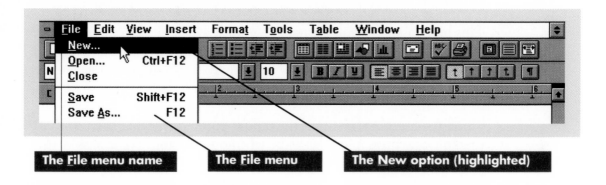

That's all you need to know to begin. So what are you waiting for?

PART ONE

What Do I Do First?

If you are new to word processors, or to Microsoft Word for Windows specifically, it may seem as if there are limitless commands, terms, techniques, clicks, what have you, that you're going to have to learn before you can really do anything. Not so! Almost everything you will ever do with Word comes down to a few very straightforward steps. In this part, you will go through the absolute basics of word processing with Word for Windows. You will learn to start the program, type something, save what you have written, print it out, and quit. What could be simpler?

5 MINUTES

Starting Word

1

To use a program, you have to start it first. Starting Word is easy. After you've done it once, you probably won't think about it again. I'll start from the first thing you might see on the screen, and tell you what to do from there.

Here We Go...

First of all, look at your screen. If it is blank, make sure your computer is on. If the screen is blank and the computer is on, you may have to turn the monitor on also. Look for a button below the picture tube, along the sides of the monitor, or in the back.

If Windows is already running, you can skip step 1 below. On the screen you should see something called the DOS prompt.

```
C:\>
```

This is a typical prompt. Yours may be C:> or D:\> or another variation. Prompts almost always end with >. It doesn't really matter much, because you're about to start Windows, and the whole point of Windows is that you don't have to think about things like prompts and memorized commands.

1. Type **WIN** and press ↵. Windows should start. Sit tight; it may take a minute.

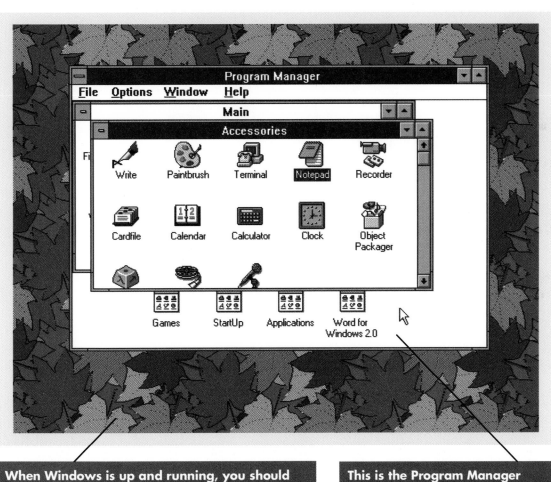

When Windows is up and running, you should see something like this. Your screen may look different in any number of ways. That's okay.

This is the Program Manager window. You'll use it to run Word.

If you don't see the Program Manager window open on your screen, look for the Program Manager icon at the bottom of the screen.

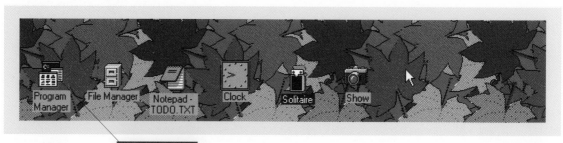

Here it is.

If you see the Program Manager icon, double-click on it to open the Program Manager window.

2. Now pull down the <u>W</u>indow menu, and see if there is a menu option that reads **Word for Windows 2.0**. If so, select it, as shown. If not, select **Applications** or **Windows Applications**.

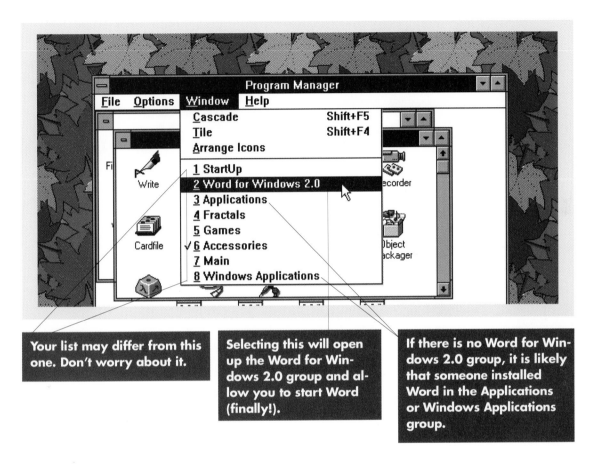

Your list may differ from this one. Don't worry about it.

Selecting this will open up the Word for Windows 2.0 group and allow you to start Word (finally!).

If there is no Word for Windows 2.0 group, it is likely that someone installed Word in the Applications or Windows Applications group.

In this window, you should see a Microsoft Word icon.

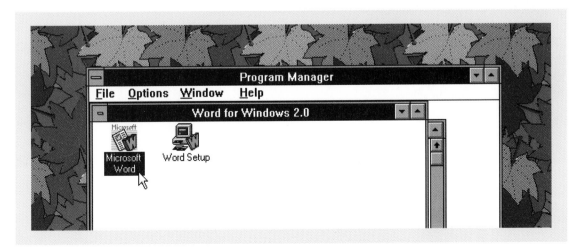

Quick & Easy

3. Double-click on the Microsoft Word icon and Word for
Windows will start.

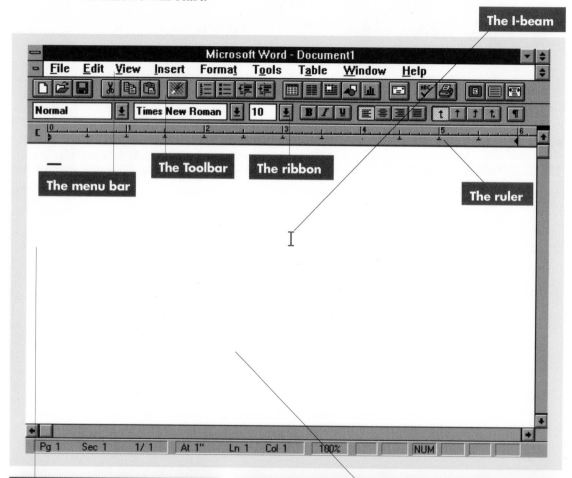

The I-beam

The Toolbar   **The ribbon**

The menu bar

The ruler

First you'll see a box showing
whom the program is registered
to and giving a bunch of licens-
ing information and other stuff
you can safely ignore. Then
you'll see this screen. This is the
moment we've been waiting for.

As you can see, almost everything on the Word for
Windows screen has a name. It can all seem a lot
more complicated than it really is. You could read a
long, boring discussion of each of these parts of
the screen, but instead, in the next lesson, you'll
jump right in and start typing, and I'll explain anything you need to know as you go along.

And that's it for preliminaries. Now you can actually do something. In
the next lesson, you'll start right in with some typing.

2

A Glorified Typewriter

or all its fancy bells and whistles, Word for Windows mainly allows you to use your computer (plus printer) as a typewriter. A very flexible typewriter, perhaps, but a typewriter nonetheless. So now it's time to do some typing.

Typing

Let's start with a simple, short example, a memo.

1. Begin by typing the first lines of a standard memo. Use your own name or make one up if you like. (Hit ↵ at the end of each line.)

MEMORANDUM ↵
To: [Tab] All Staff ↵
From: [Tab] Christian Crumlish ↵
Date: [Tab] February 27, 1994 ↵
Subject: [Tab] Four-day work week ↵

> **● Note** Don't worry about making mistakes. We're just doing typing for now. You'll learn all about how to make corrections and changes, but first things first.

2. Now, to skip a line, hit ↵ again.

3. Type the following paragraph, but don't press ↵ when you get near the end of a line. Just keep typing. You'll see why.

As you all know, we have been experimenting for the past month with a four-day work week. I am pleased to announce that the preliminary results are in, and so far the experiment has been an amazing success. Productivity is off the scale!

Your screen should now look something like this:

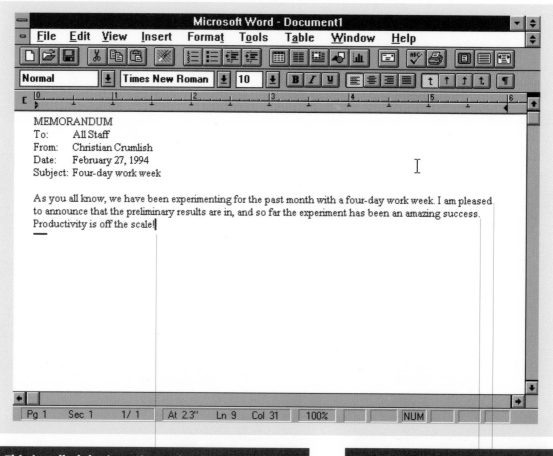

This is called the insertion point. It moves along as you type, showing where the next character will appear.

Your lines may break between different words. It's nothing to worry about.

> **● Note** You have just seen one of the advantages Word offers over a typewriter, something called "word wrap." You don't need to decide when a line is full, and you don't have to worry about going "off the paper." Just type away and watch the words "wrap" from one line to the next. Use ↵ only to end paragraphs or to leave blank lines.

4. Press ↵ twice to start a new paragraph.

5. Type the following:

I'm sure I'm not the only one here who used to dread Monday morning, but I think you'll all agree that it looks a lot brighter after a three-day weekend. Because of the success of our trial run, we are going to extend the four-day work week schedule for a further six months. If all goes well, and I don't see any reason why it shouldn't, we'll make the plan permanent. ⤶

Your screen should look like this:

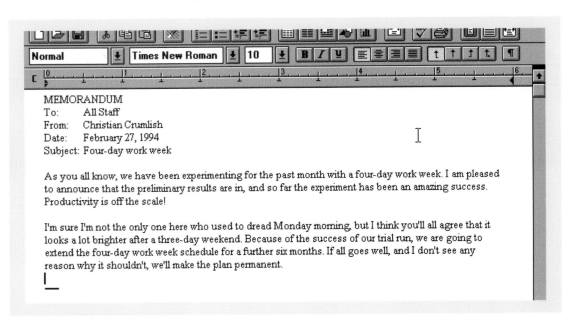

There, now you've made a document, but putting words down on the page or the screen is often just the first step. A first draft on a computer screen has a way of looking finished just because the letters are set in type and the lines are all even, but often you'll need to revise a draft, possibly more than once. Word for Windows provides a variety of editing tools and techniques, but the easiest to use, and the ones you'll take advantage of most often, are the Backspace and Delete keys.

When to Use Backspace and When to Use Delete

You'll use Backspace most of the time to make corrections on the fly. I'll take you through the process once, step by step, but you'll see that it quickly becomes second nature, and, if you're a sloppy typist, like me, it becomes part of the typing process itself.

1. Press ↵ to skip a line.

2. Type **Next experiment is telecommuting** and stop there.

3. Press Backspace thirteen times. Watch as the insertion point moves backward, eating up the word *telecommuting* one letter at a time.

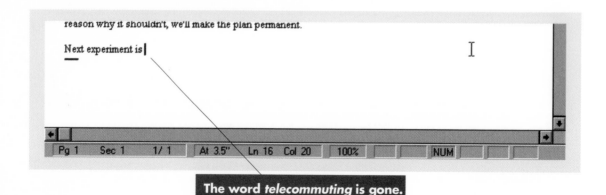

reason why it shouldn't, we'll make the plan permanent.

Next experiment is

Pg 1   Sec 1   1/1   At 3.5"   Ln 16   Col 20   100%   NUM

The word *telecommuting* is gone.

4. In place of the erased word, type **working at home.** (including the period).

5. Hit ↵.

So you see, pressing **Backspace** erases the character to the *left* of the insertion point. This doesn't necessarily mean the letter you just typed.

6. Using the mouse, move the I-beam so it is positioned exactly between the *N* and *e* in *Next*.

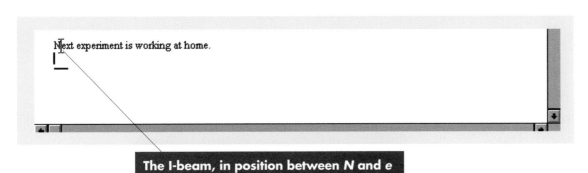

The I-beam, in position between *N* and *e*

7. Click the mouse. The insertion point appears where you clicked.

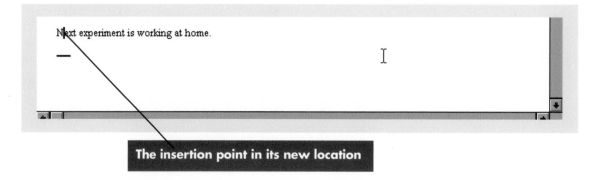

The insertion point in its new location

8. Press **Backspace** once.

9. Type **The n**. (Don't type the period, it's one of mine.)

The difference between **Backspace** and **Delete** is that the Delete key erases the character to the *right* of the insertion point.

10. Put the insertion point just before the *w* in *working*.

11. Hit **Delete** repeatedly until the rest of the line disappears.

● Note You can also just hold down **Delete** and it will delete many characters very quickly. This can sometimes be risky because you may erase something you didn't mean to. In this case, however, you're already at the end of the memo, so the worst thing that might happen is you might hear some warning beeps that tell you you've reached the end and there's nothing more to delete. By the way, **Backspace** and many other keys also repeat this way when you hold them down. You might as well throw that old Selectric away.

12. Type **telecommuting.** (including the period) and then press ↵. (Well, I had to change it to something.)

The next experiment is telecommuting.

So, to erase a word with Backspace, put the insertion point at the end of the word. To erase a word with Delete, put the insertion point at the beginning.

If you plan to take a break before continuing, first take the time to save your memo, as explained in Lesson 3. Then, when you feel like doing some more, check Lesson 7 for how to reopen the memo and continue where you left off.

15 MINUTES

Save or You'll Be Sorry

3

One good reason to use a computer for writing is that the computer has a memory. It can store your work and you can return to it later. But the computer does not automatically remember what you do, and just because you see something on the screen is no guarantee it will be there later when you come back to it.

That's why you have to *save* your work. It's very easy to do. I'll show you that, and then I'll also show you how to save something to a floppy disk, so you can take your work from one computer to another.

Finally, I'll show you a good way to have Word save automatically, so that in case of an accident or emergency, you won't lose all the work you've done since the last time you saved.

But first, regular everyday saving.

Saving Your Document for the First Time

Here's how to save the memo you typed in Lesson 2:

1. Pull down the File menu and select Save, as shown:

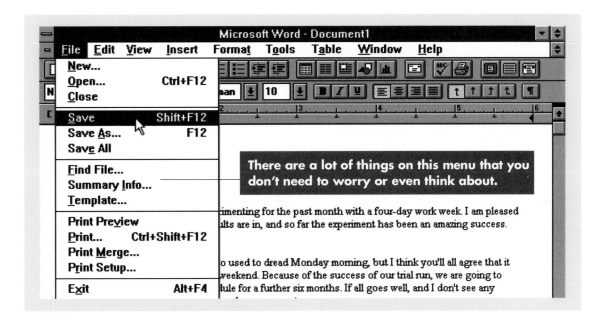

There are a lot of things on this menu that you don't need to worry or even think about.

You'll see the following dialog box appear:

This is the directory Word for Windows is in. If winword is not highlighted on your screen, double-click on it. If you don't see winword, double-click on c:\ (or perhaps d:\) at the top of the list, and then double-click on winword.

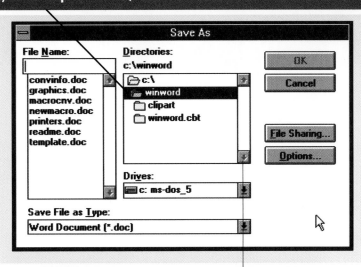

You may need to click this arrow to see the rest of the list. (This is called "scrolling.")

> **● Note** As usual, there are all sorts of buttons and things in this dialog box that may make you queasy. Just ignore them, at least for now.

2. You have to give your document a name. Type **memo** (under File <u>N</u>ame:) in the dialog box:

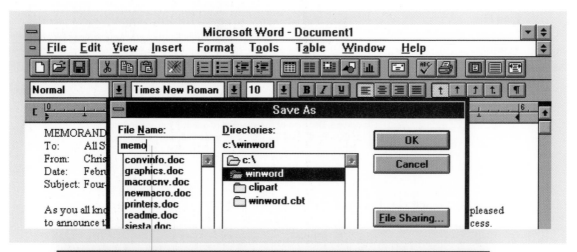

If you're typing and nothing's happening in this box, hit Tab a few times until you see the insertion point appear here. Your memo will be saved in the WINWORD directory. Eventually you may want to create a special directory for Word documents, but for now, this should be fine.

3. Click the OK button.

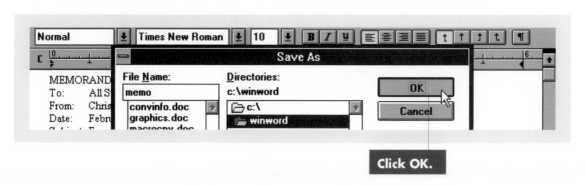

Click OK.

● Note You could also press ↵. With any dialog box, if you hit the Enter key, it's just the same as if you clicked whichever button is highlighted. In this case it's the OK button. This also means that you must be careful *not* to press ↵ before you are finished entering information in a dialog box.

You see yet another dialog box:

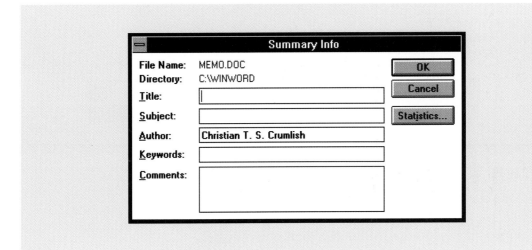

4. If this is your copy of Word for Windows, you'll see your name in the Author box. If not, hit Tab until the name in the box is highlighted and then type your name in its place. You can safely ignore the rest of the information.

5. Click OK.

There, you've saved your memo. The name you gave it is now in the title bar:

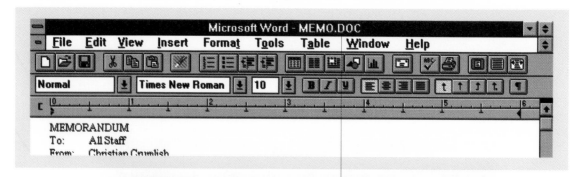

Notice that Word has given your memo the extension .DOC, which identifies it as a Word for Windows document.

Saving Changes to a Document

If you make changes to your document, you'll need to save it again. Otherwise, the changes will be lost forever. To learn how to do this, make a minor change to the memo and then save it again.

1. Make sure the insertion point is at the end of the memo by hitting PageDown.

2. Press ↵ to add another blank line to the memo. This doesn't really change the way the memo looks, but it is a real change.

3. Pull down the File menu and select Save.

Word saves your document again, in a flash. If you blink, you'll miss it. And if you watch very carefully, the only thing you'll see is the status bar at the bottom of the screen as it first tells you that it's saving and then shows how many words are in your document.

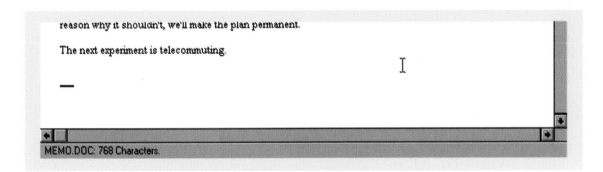

reason why it shouldn't, we'll make the plan permanent.

The next experiment is telecommuting.

MEMO.DOC: 768 Characters.

Saving a Copy of Your Document

There are several reasons why you might want to make a copy of your document. If you plan to make a similar document, you can save a copy of the first and then change the copy while keeping the original unchanged. Or, if you need to work on your document on another machine, perhaps to print it out, you'll have to save a copy of the document to a floppy disk, and then carry the disk to the other computer. If you don't have your own computer to work on, you'll usually need to save your work to a disk so that you can keep it. It's also good to keep copies of your work on disks in case there are ever problems with your computer or its hard disk, which is where your work is stored. Now I'll show you how to save a copy of your memo to a disk.

1. Get a floppy disk and insert it in the disk drive. (If you have more than one, insert it in the upper drive or the left-most one.) If there is a latch or door on the drive, close it.

2. Pull down the File menu and select Save As, as shown:

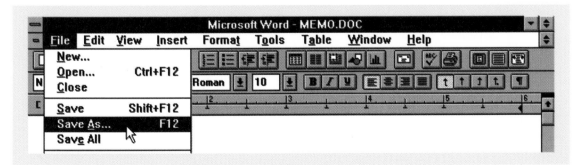

You'll see the same dialog box you saw the first time you saved this memo.

3. Click the down arrow in the Dri<u>v</u>es box, and select the a: drive, as shown:

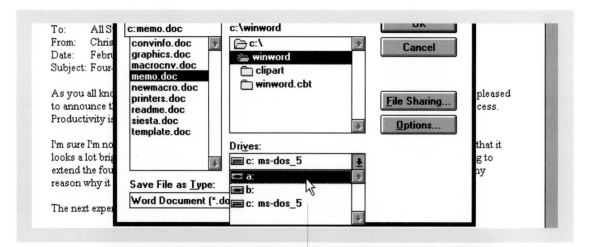

This is a drop-down list box. (What a mouthful!) Yours may not show drive b:, or it may show drive d:.

• Note If your computer has two disk drives and you've put your disk in the second (lower or rightmost) drive, then you'll need to select the b: drive. It's okay if you selected a: first; you'll just have to pull down the list of drives again.

4. Click OK. (You could give the file a new name first, if you wanted to, but why bother?) The Summary Info dialog box appears again.

5. Click OK (again). Word saves your memo to the floppy disk.

Word has now forgotten about the first copy of your memo, which is all right, but you have to be aware that, for instance, if you save the memo after making changes, you'll be saving the changes to the copy on the disk. (And if you've taken the disk out of the drive, Word will get confused.) So remember to use Save As again, next time, instead of Save, and specify the c: drive again. (The c: drive is your hard disk. That's where the memo was saved originally.)

The Automatic Save Insurance Policy

One of the scariest things about computers, especially for beginners, is wondering what can go wrong. At least with pen and paper, or with a typewriter, your words are not going to just vanish from the page. Unfortunately, disasters do happen. Any disaster—a power outage, a hard-disk crash, or even someone tripping on the power cord and pulling it out of the wall—has the same effect. You lose all the work you've done, *since the last time you saved.* Believe me, it's better to learn the lesson of saving regularly the easy way, because if you don't, eventually you'll learn it the hard way.

That's why I recommend taking out a little insurance policy against disaster. It's called automatic save. What it does is save your work for you at regular intervals. Here's how to do it.

1. Pull down the <u>F</u>ile menu and select Save <u>A</u>s.

2. Click the <u>O</u>ptions button on the right side of the dialog box, as shown:

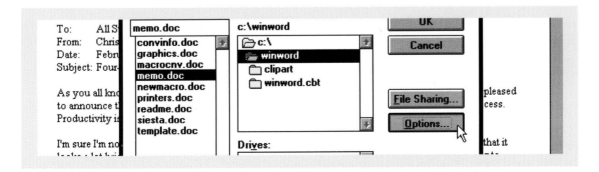

3. This brings up yet another dialog box. Click on Automatic Save Every. The check box next to it will be filled in with an ×.

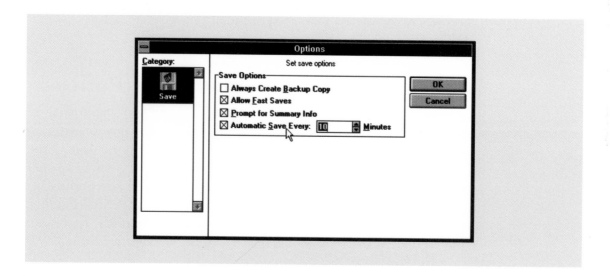

4. Type **15**. It will replace the 10 in the Minutes box.

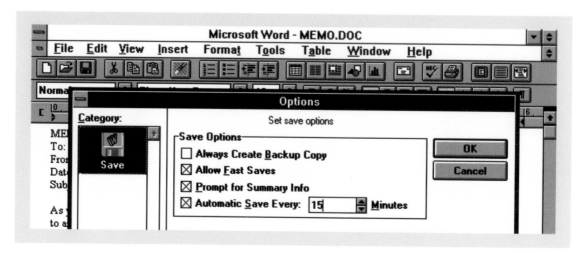

Word suggests automatic saving every 10 minutes, but every 15 minutes is probably safe. (Think of it this way: In case of a disaster, how much work will you want to redo? The only reason not to make Word save your work every minute is that saving takes a little bit of time and this could slow you down.)

5. Click OK. You are now back at the Save As dialog box.

6. Click Close (not OK, unless you want to save your document at this moment).

Now your work will be safe even if something really bad happens. If you do have a disaster at some point (knock wood), just run Word again, and it will retrieve the last automatically saved copy of your document.

Printing the Easy Way

4

In some ways, printing is the most important feature of any word processor. What good is word wrap, editing, or computer memory if you can't get your work printed out on paper? As with most of its features, Word for Windows allows you all kinds of control over the printing process, but most of it is overkill, as usual. In this lesson I'll show you how to cut to the chase when it comes to printing, by taking advantage of one of Word's genuinely useful new features, the Toolbar.

One-Step Printing

The buttons on the Toolbar are all shortcuts. Each one of them stands for a command that you could select by pulling down the appropriate menu and choosing the proper option. Some are more useful than others. The Print button is one of the more useful ones because it really does save you a step or two.

The buttons are *icons,* meaning that they show symbols instead of words. You're supposed to be able to look at any of them and tell what they mean. Don't feel stupid if they're not all crystal clear to you—that's the way it is with icons. Often they're obvious only to the programmers who designed them. The Print button is fourth from the right and has a little picture of what looks like a laser printer on it.

Here, let me get my magnifying glass:

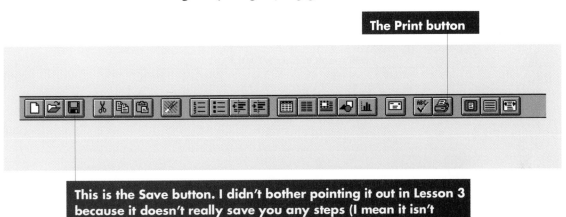

The Print button

This is the Save button. I didn't bother pointing it out in Lesson 3 because it doesn't really save you any steps (I mean it isn't really any faster than choosing Save on the File menu).

To make a long story short (I know, I've been doing the opposite), here's the one step I promised:

1. Click the Print button.

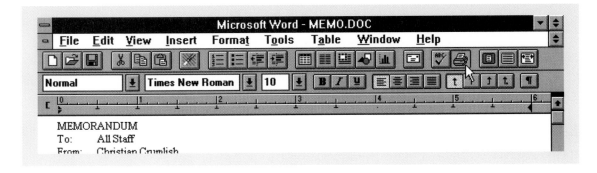

Quick & Easy

You'll see a dialog box like the following as Word prints your entire document:

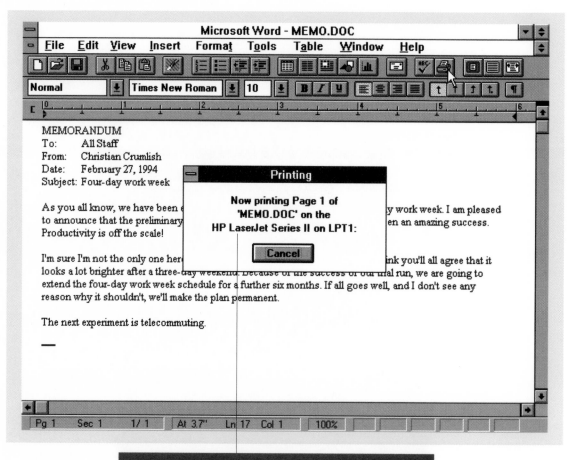

The name of your printer (that is, the printer your computer is hooked up to) is right here.

● Note If you have second thoughts at the last minute, you can click the Cancel button in the dialog box, but a document as short as the memo you've been working on will already have been whisked to the printer, so it's not really worth the bother. (Of course, if you want to cancel the printing of a 50-page report, that's the way to do it.)

Isn't that simple? Here's how the memo looks printed out on an HP LaserJet II:

MEMORANDUM
To: All Staff
From: Christian Crumlish
Date: February 27, 1994
Subject: Four-day work week

As you all know, we have been experimenting for the past month with a four-day work week. I am pleased to announce that the preliminary results are in, and so far the experiment has been an amazing success. Productivity is off the scale!

I'm sure I'm not the only one here who used to dread Monday morning, but I think you'll all agree that it looks a lot brighter after a three-day weekend. Because of the success of our trial run, we are going to extend the four-day work week schedule for a further six months. If all goes well, and I don't see any reason why it shouldn't, we'll make the plan permanent.

The next experiment is telecommuting.

If your memo printed out okay, then you're done with this lesson. If you've run into a snag, there are a few easy things you can check.

No Fair! My Document Didn't Print Out!

If you followed my instruction but nothing came out of the printer, it could be a simple problem, easily fixed, or it might be something more complicated, in which case your best bet would be to call in your local guru to take a look. I'll tell you the simple things to check.

The most common problem in printing is that the printer is turned off or is *off-line,* which means "not ready to print." Another possible source of the problem is that the cables that connect the printer to your computer are detached or have come loose. Word may or may not alert you to any of these problems. That is, your screen may show the dialog box I illustrated, just as if the memo really were printing, even though nothing comes out of the printer. Or, you could get the following dialog box on the screen:

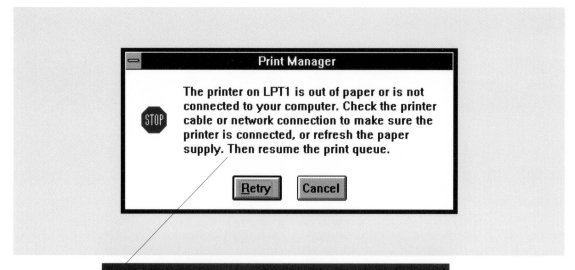

Print Manager

The printer on LPT1 is out of paper or is not connected to your computer. Check the printer cable or network connection to make sure the printer is connected, or refresh the paper supply. Then resume the print queue.

STOP

[Retry]   [Cancel]

Word is trying to tell you what the problem is. You can click Retry, but chances are you'll end up back here again with this dialog box on the screen.

Either way, the first thing to do is to make sure your printer is turned on. Every printer has an On/Off switch somewhere prominent, so just look around and you'll see it. Next, make sure the printer is on-line. Look for a button that says "Select," or "ON LINE." If there's a little message window, the message in it should be "Ready."

Look and see if the printer is out of paper. If it is, insert some (or ask someone who knows how). You can also check that the cables going into the printer are snug in their ports (sockets), both at the printer and at the computer end. If it looks like the printer is turned on, on-line, and well connected to your computer, try turning the printer (not the computer!) off, wait a few seconds, and then turn it on again. (This is called "power cycling" if you're trying to impress someone with your jargon.) You'd be amazed how often this simple trick gets things rolling again.

If you think you've corrected what was wrong, click Retry. Your final resort, if all else fails, is to make sure that the proper printer is selected. (This is something you *can't* do with the Print button.)

1. Pull down the File menu and select Print Setup, as shown:

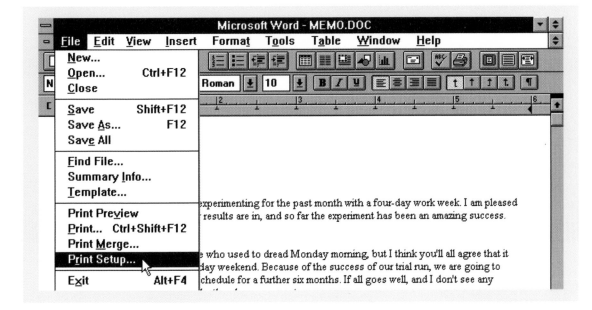

You'll see this dialog box:

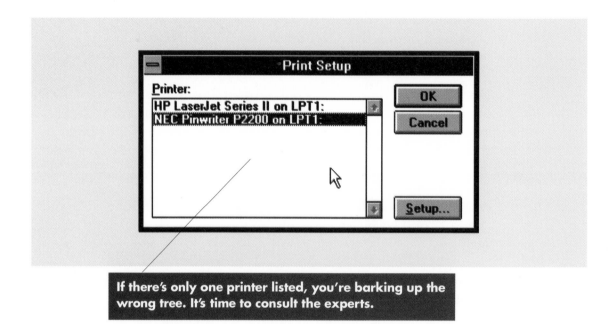

If there's only one printer listed, you're barking up the wrong tree. It's time to consult the experts.

This method is only going to help you if the list shows more than one printer *and* the one highlighted is not the one you were trying to print to. (If you are unfamiliar with the name of your printer, look at it—the name should be there in the front somewhere.)

2. If the wrong printer *is* highlighted, double-click on the name of the correct printer, as shown:

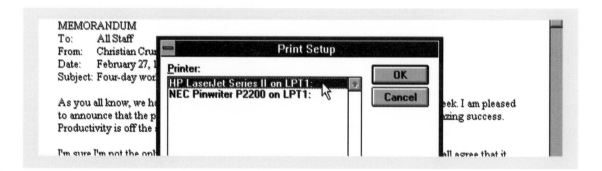

3. Click the Print button again, and cross your fingers.

If none of this advice helps and you're tearing your hair out, you really should consult someone who knows your setup and has some experience with troubleshooting. Printers are notoriously fickle, but most of the problems that can arise aren't too difficult to solve.

When You Got to Go, You Got to Go

5

When you've finished what you're working on, or if you've had enough for one sitting, you can't just turn off your computer. First, you have to quit Word for Windows. This is a very easy thing to do, so this lesson will be short.

Exiting Is Your Last Chance to Save

If you've been taking my advice so far, you've been saving your document whenever you make changes to it, so you don't have to worry about losing your work. In case you forget, Word provides a safety net. When you try to leave the program, it checks to see if you've made any changes since the last time you saved, and if you have, it gives you one final chance to save your work before quitting.

Before the last time you saved the memo, you added a blank line at the end of it. Delete that line now to see what happens when you try to exit Word.

1. Press **PageDown** to make sure the insertion point is at the end of the document.

2. Press **Delete** once.

3. Pull down the File menu and select Exit, as shown:

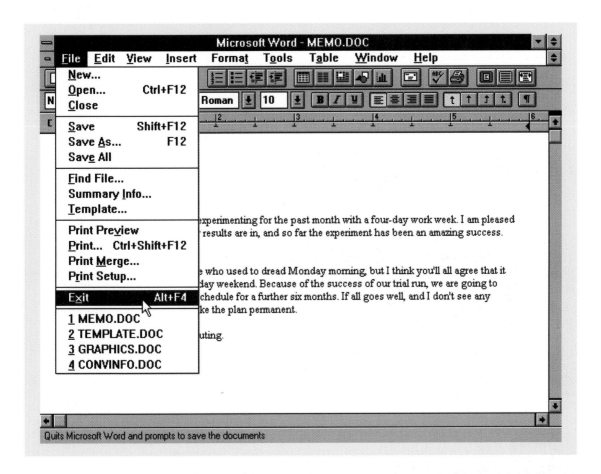

This dialog box appears:

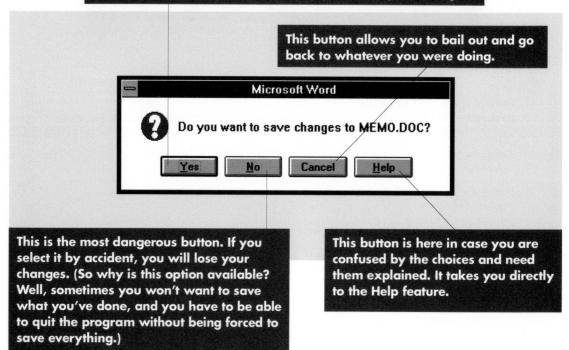

Word assumes that you probably *do* want to save your changes (usually a good bet), so this button is the default, which means that if you press ↵, Word will save your changes.

This button allows you to bail out and go back to whatever you were doing.

Microsoft Word

Do you want to save changes to MEMO.DOC?

Yes | No | Cancel | Help

This is the most dangerous button. If you select it by accident, you will lose your changes. (So why is this option available? Well, sometimes you won't want to save what you've done, and you have to be able to quit the program without being forced to save everything.)

This button is here in case you are confused by the choices and need them explained. It takes you directly to the Help feature.

● Note If you are working with more than one document (something I'll discuss in Part Two), you'll be given these choices for each document with unsaved changes.

4. Click the <u>Y</u>es button.

If you have not previously saved your document (unlike MEMO.DOC), you will be taken to the Save As dialog box described in Lesson 3, and you can then give your document a name and save it. If your document already has a name (as is the case with MEMO.DOC), Word will save your most recent changes as soon as you click Yes.

After Word saves your changes, it shuts down and returns you to Windows.

You can quit Windows and return to DOS by pulling down the Program Manager's File menu and selecting Exit Windows. Click OK in the dialog box that appears.

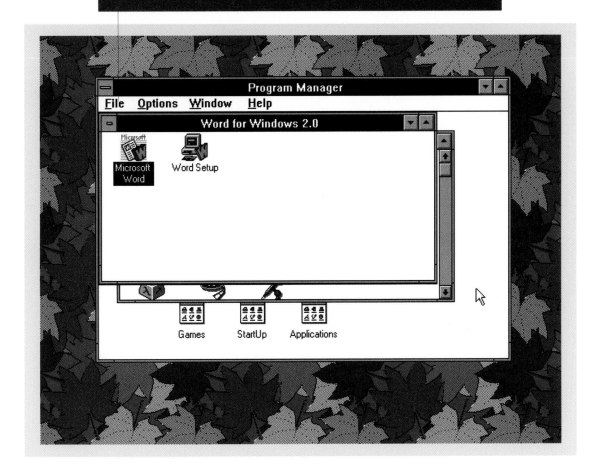

So that's what happens when you quit with unsaved changes. If you exit without having made any unsaved changes, no dialog box appears. Word just quits and returns you to Windows.

PART TWO

Getting Things into Shape

If you've worked your way through Part One, then you've written at least one simple document. You now know the basics of word processing with Word. In this part, I'll discuss the various ways you might want to improve the appearance of your document. You could get by just fine with what you already know, when it comes to getting words down on the page. But the usual purpose of writing is communication, and if you want people to read what you've written, it pays to shape up your document. I'll show you how to make some text stand out from the rest, how to control where the words appear on the page, and how to make a title page for a formal document. The first thing you'll learn is how to return to a document you've already written.

Picking Up Where You Left Off

6

Okay, so you've written something. Your words are stored on your computer's disk. You have *hard copy*, meaning a copy of your document printed out on paper, but you realize that you'd like to fiddle around with it a little bit—see if you can make it look better. So where do you start? Well, the first thing you'll need to do is open up your document, that is to say, have Word find your document on the disk and display it on the screen so you can continue working with it. As soon as you successfully open your document, go on to the next lesson.

The Easy Way to Reopen Your Document

Word for Windows keeps track of the last four documents you (or anyone else) worked on. Unless a lot of water has gone under the bridge since the last time you saw your document, it will be listed at the bottom of the File menu. (If you need to start Word and you forget how, refer to Lesson 1.)

1. Pull down the <u>F</u>ile menu and select **MEMO.DOC**, as shown:

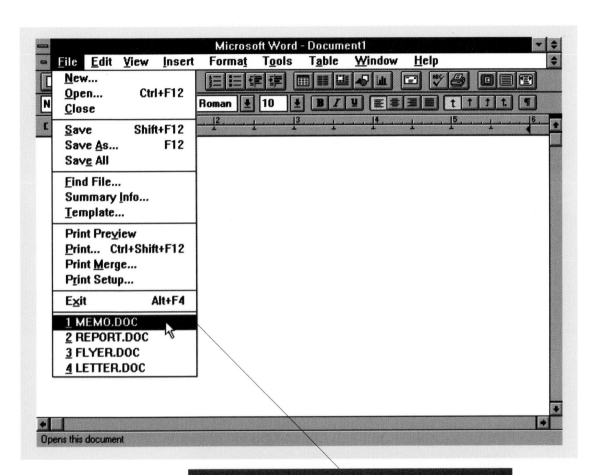

Look at the bottom of the menu to make sure that MEMO.DOC is listed. (On my menu, you can also see the three other documents that I've worked on most recently. Of course, your list will differ.) If MEMO.DOC is not on your list, skip to the next section of this lesson without selecting anything on this menu.

Word retrieves your memo and displays it on the screen.

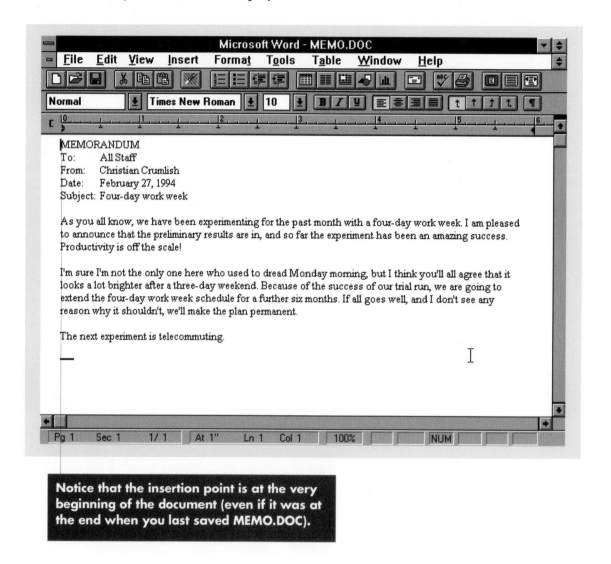

Notice that the insertion point is at the very beginning of the document (even if it was at the end when you last saved MEMO.DOC).

So that's the easy way. But even if your document has been replaced on the File menu by more recent ones, the steps for finding and retrieving it are pretty simple. (If you successfully opened MEMO just now, you can skip the next section.)

Right Where You Left It

Whether or not you remember exactly where your document is, the procedure to open it is about the same:

1. Pull down the File menu and select Open, as shown:

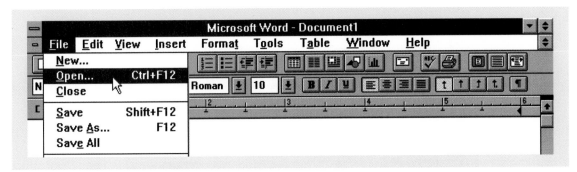

This dialog box will appear:

You are now looking at documents in this directory. In my case it's c:\winword. This has to match the directory you saved your document to.

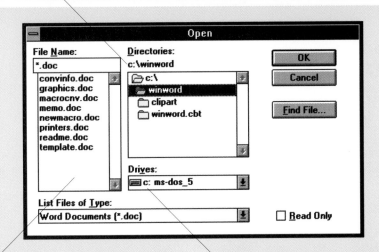

This is a list box, where the list of Word documents appears. You look here for the document you are trying to open.

You are looking at documents in a directory on this disk. In my case it's the c: disk, the main one.

Quick & Easy

2. If you see **memo.doc** in the file list, double-click it, as
shown:

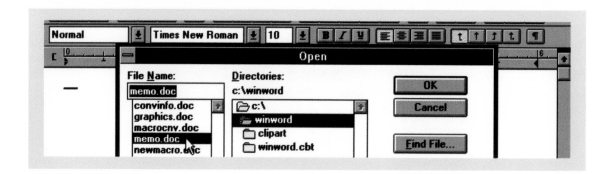

Word will retrieve your memo, and you're all set. If you did not see
your document on the list, I'll help you find it.

What to Do
If Your Document Is Hiding

If the list box is filled with the names of other documents, then the first
thing you should try is scrolling the list.

1. Click below the scroll box in the little scroll bar at the right
side of the list box, as shown:

If you still don't see your document in this list box
after clicking once, you may need to click again.
When you have reached the end of the list, the
scroll box will be at the bottom of the scroll bar.

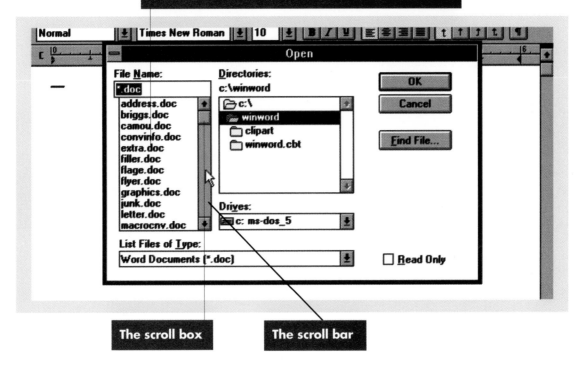

The scroll box   The scroll bar

2. As you reveal the rest of the list, continue looking for
memo.doc. If you see it, double-click on it.

If you still don't see it, that means your current directory (the one
shown under <u>D</u>irectories to the right of the list box) must not be WIN-
WORD. (Remember, you saved the memo to the WINWORD direc-
tory in Lesson 3.)

Quick & Easy

3. Double-click on **winword** in the <u>D</u>irectories list box, as
shown:

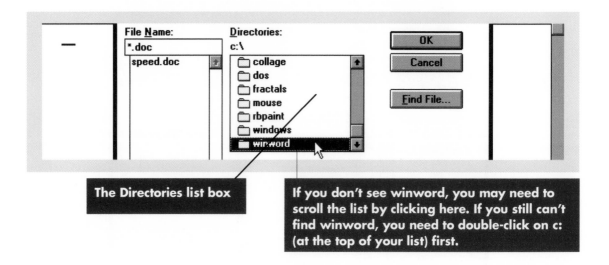

The Directories list box

If you don't see winword, you may need to
scroll the list by clicking here. If you still can't
find winword, you need to double-click on c:
(at the top of your list) first.

4. Look through the list for **memo.doc** and double-click on it.

7

Starting Something New

So now you've got MEMO.DOC on the screen. You've learned how to return to something where you left off. But what do you do if you want to work on something new? Remember, to write your first document, you just started typing—the screen was blank. But now, imagine you've finished working on one document or project, and you want to start some other project. You can start a new document without getting rid of the old one. In this lesson, I'll show you how.

The Easiest Way to Start a New Document

You'll like this. It's just one step:

1. Click the leftmost icon on the Toolbar, as shown:

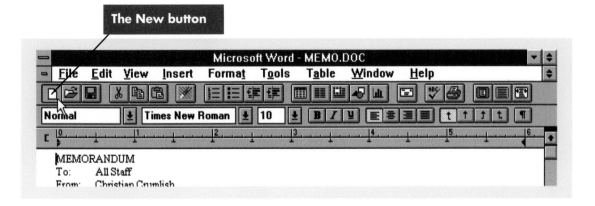

The New button

Quick & Easy

● Note There is a New command on the File menu, but using the button
is faster and saves you a step.

Instantly, Word starts a new document for you and the typing area is
cleared.

In the title bar, your new document is called Document2 for now.
Whenever you start Word, the empty document you begin with
is called Document1 until you give it a name. Any new documents you start are called Document2, Document3, etc.

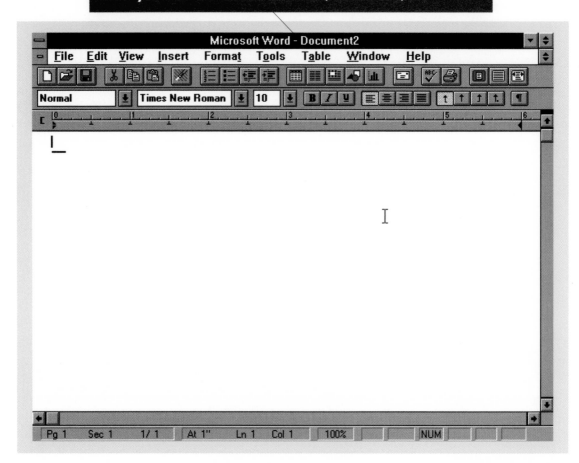

You're ready to begin typing a new document.

What Happened to My First Document?

You may now be wondering what happened to MEMO.DOC. Don't worry. It's still there—you just can't see it right now. Try this:

1. Pull down the <u>W</u>indow menu and select MEMO.DOC, like so:

This menu shows you all your open documents. This is the easiest way to switch between them.

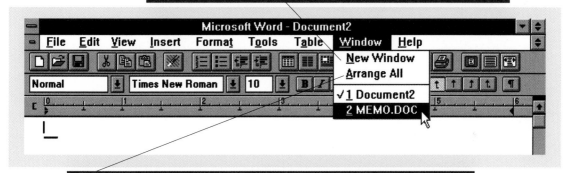

This command allows you to see all your documents at once, but they appear in small windows (the more documents you have open, the smaller they need to be), so it's often not very useful.

Look familiar? It works both ways.

2. Pull down the <u>W</u>indow menu and select Document2, like so:

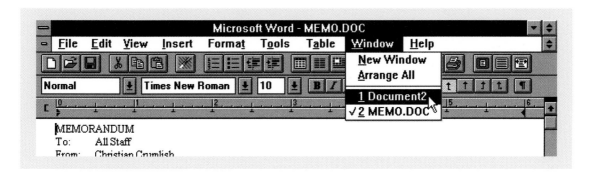

47

That's all there is to switching between open documents.

A Larger Sample Document

In the rest of Part Two, you will learn how to emphasize text and control the appearance of your pages. You probably won't need to fiddle much with short documents like the memo you typed. That's why I'd like you to have a longer document to work with, in fact one that covers several pages. A report is a typical example. Of course, I don't expect you to type pages and pages of my entertaining prose, so I'll give you a little bit to begin with and then you'll fake the rest.

1. Type this title, subtitle, and a name (yours, mine, or a made-up one):

Midday Siestas and Workers' Productivity ⏎
A Proposal ⏎
Christian Crumlish ⏎
Department of Human Resources ⏎

2. Now, press ⏎ twice to skip two lines. Your screen should look like this:

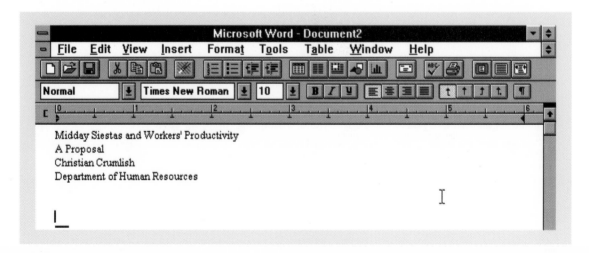

3. Type the following report opener (remember, don't press ↵ until you get to the end of the paragraph):

In many of the more southerly countries it is well known that a person can get more work done and enjoy work, and indeed life, more greatly simply by taking a nap in the middle of the day. In Spanish-speaking countries this is known as a siesta. There's more than one way to skin a rat and there's more than one way to divide up eight hours. ↵

Now you need a dummy paragraph to fill out the rest of the report.

4. Press ↵ to insert a blank line.

5. Type this paragraph (I promise this is the last one):

The words in this paragraph are all filler. Repeated many times, they will give the appearance of a full-length document. On and on the paragraph rambles, drifting further and further into random-sounding strings of words. Of course, it doesn't really have to say anything. As long as it looks like a typical paragraph, it will do. Another sentence or two and it will be long enough. Just one more and it will be perfect! There, that ought to do it. ↵

Your screen should look something like this:

Quick&Easy

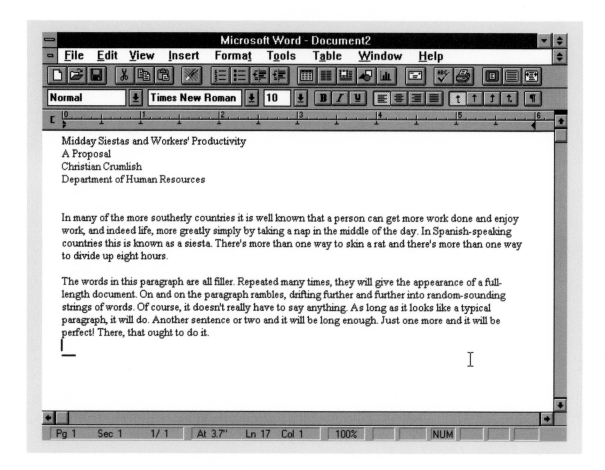

I'm sure that's enough typing for you. To avoid typing all day, you're going to copy this paragraph a bunch of times to give the appearance of a longer document.

● Note To build this large document, I'm asking you to do some things without much explanation. I'll explain more about procedures like copying and pasting in Part Three. But first things first.

6. Press ↑ five times to move the insertion point to the left of the *T* in *The* at the beginning of the paragraph.

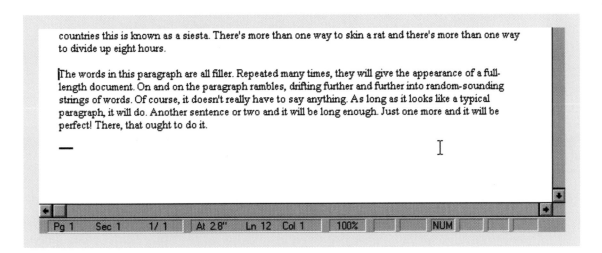

7. Hold down **Shift** and press **PageDown**. The entire paragraph is selected (including the blank line at the end).

8. Click the fifth button on the Toolbar, the one that shows two miniature documents.

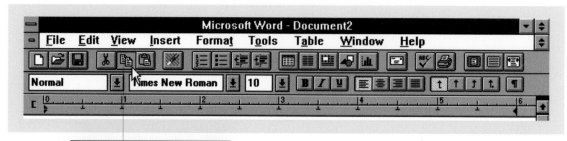

This is the Copy button.

9. Press PageDown and then ↵.

10. Now click the sixth button, the one with a miniature clip-board and tiny piece of paper on it:

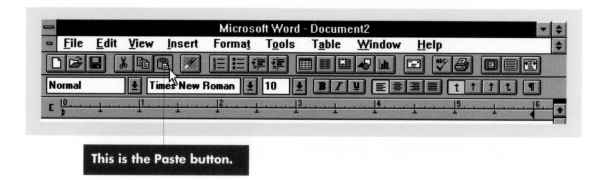

This is the Paste button.

The dummy paragraph is copied once.

11. Click the Copy button 16 times (or so); the dummy paragraph is repeated over and over.

Your screen should look something like this:

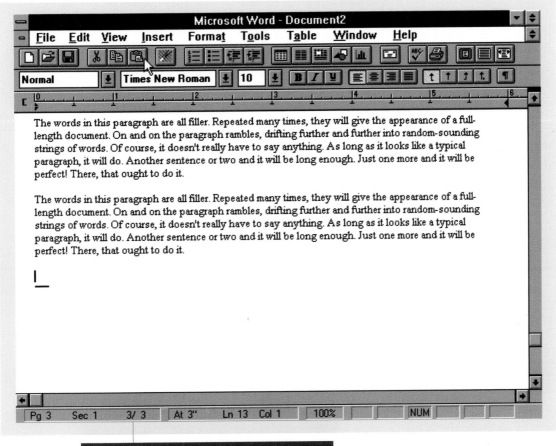

These numbers mean that you are on
page 3 out of 3 pages total.

So now you have a long document. Save it as **SIESTA** in the
WINWORD directory. (Refer to Lesson 3 if you need a reminder
of how to save.)

15 MINUTES

Finding Your Way Around

8

With a long document, such as SIESTA, which you just created in Lesson 7, you can only see part of it on the screen at any time. So there are a few things you ought to know about getting from one part of a document to another. In this lesson I'll show you how to move the insertion point anywhere you want and how to scroll through a document. If you've exited since the last lesson, open SIESTA before continuing. You learned to open a document in Lesson 6.

Giant Steps

You've already learned about some of the common ways to move the insertion point. One way is to position the I-beam with the mouse and click. But it's not always convenient to use the mouse to get around; sometimes you'd rather keep your hands close to the keyboard. Another way is to press the arrow keys, such as ↑ and →. But it can get mighty tedious hitting → five hundred times to get to the next page. There are shortcuts. Try some now.

1. Press **Ctrl-Home.** The insertion point jumps to the beginning of the document.

Notice that the scroll box is at the top of the scroll bar.

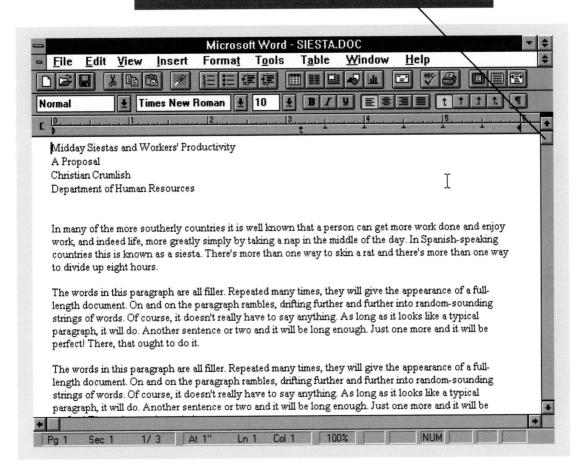

If you've just reopened SIESTA, the insertion point is already at the beginning of the document and you'll just hear a beep when you press Ctrl-Home.

2. Press Ctrl-End. The insertion point jumps back to the end of the document.

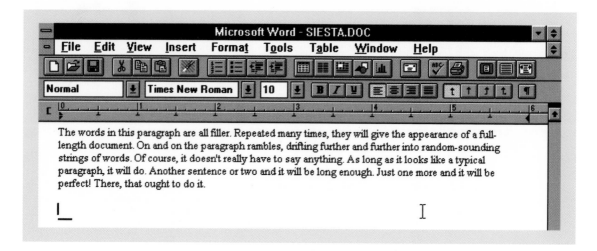

3. Press PageUp. The insertion point does not appear to move but it is now positioned one window—one screenful of text—above its previous location.

You've moved up one window, but the insertion point is in the same place on the screen.

The dotted line is the page break between page 2 and page 3.

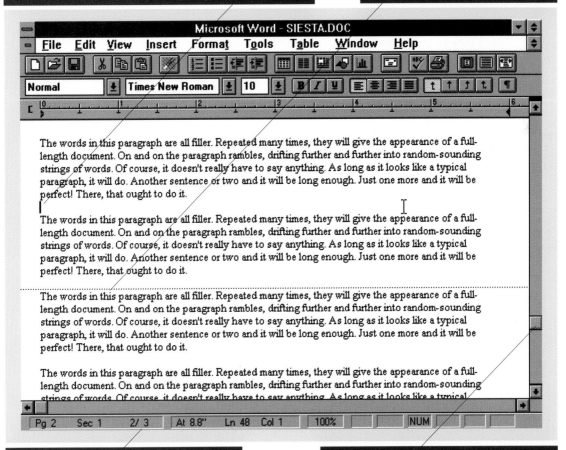

This shows that the insertion point is on page 2 of a 3-page document (it's above the page break).

The location of the scroll box in the scroll bar gives you some idea of where you are now in the document (near but not quite at the end).

Quick **Easy**

● **Note** Don't worry if your screen doesn't match mine exactly. The
important thing is that your insertion point is in the same place
on the screen—about one-third of the way down.

4. Press **Ctrl-PageUp**. The insertion point moves to the top of
the screen.

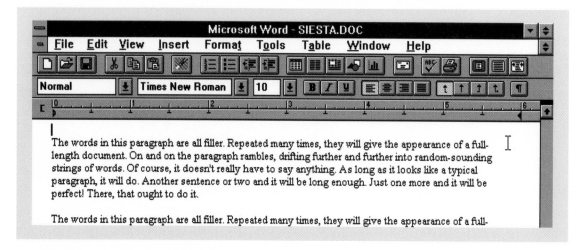

5. Press **PageUp** again. The insertion point moves up another
screenful of text. (It's still at the top of the screen, but the
text has moved down.)

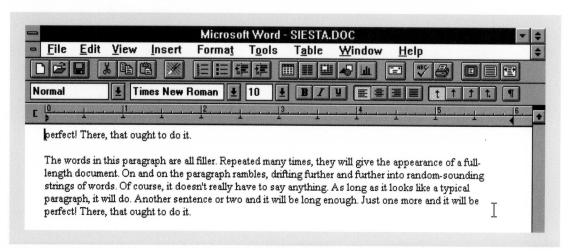

6. Press **Ctrl-PageDown**. The insertion point moves to the end of the last full line on the screen.

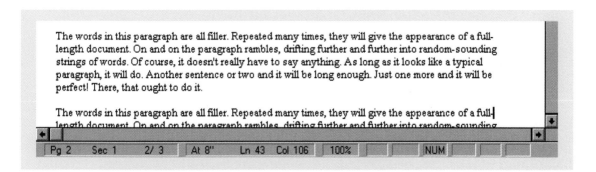

Just as **Ctrl-PageDown** does the opposite of **Ctrl-PageUp**, **PageDown** does the opposite of **PageUp**. That is, it moves the insertion point down one whole screenful of text. Now I'll show you how to get to the beginning or end of a *line of text*.

7. Press **Home**. The insertion point jumps to the beginning of the line.

strings of words. Of course, it doesn't really have to say anything. As long as it looks like a typical paragraph, it will do. Another sentence or two and it will be long enough. Just one more and it will be perfect! There, that ought to do it.

The words in this paragraph are all filler. Repeated many times, they will give the appearance of a full-length document. On and on the paragraph rambles, drifting further and further into random-sounding

| Pg 2 | Sec 1 | 2/ 3 | At 8" | Ln 43 | Col 1 | 100% | | | NUM | | | |

Col 1 means that the insertion point is located just before the first character on the line.

8. Press **End**. The insertion point returns to the end of the line.

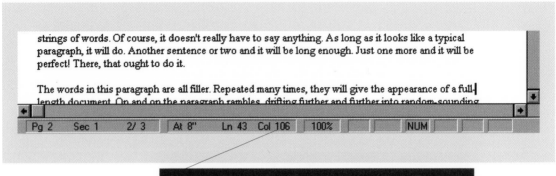

strings of words. Of course, it doesn't really have to say anything. As long as it looks like a typical paragraph, it will do. Another sentence or two and it will be long enough. Just one more and it will be perfect! There, that ought to do it.

The words in this paragraph are all filler. Repeated many times, they will give the appearance of a full-length document. On and on the paragraph rambles, drifting further and further into random-sounding

| Pg 2 | Sec 1 | 2/ 3 | At 8" | Ln 43 | Col 106 | 100% | | | | NUM | | |

Col 106 means that the insertion point is located before what would be the 106th character on the line. Count them if you're bored!

So that makes two more ways to make big jumps around your document. Now, slightly smaller steps.

One Step at a Time

You won't always want to skip to the end of your document or all the way to the end of a line. Sometimes you'll be aiming for a point just a few paragraphs down, say, or for the middle of a line.

1. Press ←. The insertion point moves to the left one character.

2. Now press **Ctrl-←**. This time the insertion point moves to the beginning of the word.

3. Press **Ctrl-←** again. The insertion point moves to the beginning of the next word to the left.

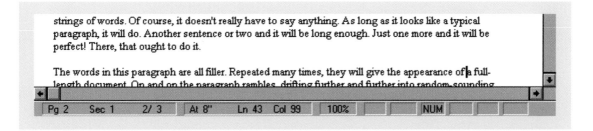

strings of words. Of course, it doesn't really have to say anything. As long as it looks like a typical paragraph, it will do. Another sentence or two and it will be long enough. Just one more and it will be perfect! There, that ought to do it.

The words in this paragraph are all filler. Repeated many times, they will give the appearance of a full-length document. On and on the paragraph rambles, drifting further and further into random-sounding

| Pg 2 | Sec 1 | 2/ 3 | At 8" | Ln 43 | Col 99 | 100% | | | NUM | | | |

4. Press **Home**. The insertion point moves to the beginning of the line.

5. Press →. The insertion point moves right one character.

6. Press **Ctrl**-→. The insertion point moves to the beginning of the next word.

7. Press **Ctrl**-→ again. The insertion point moves one more word to the right.

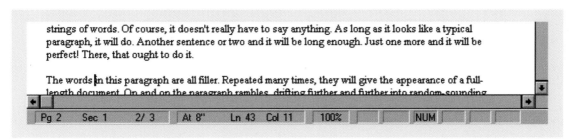

strings of words. Of course, it doesn't really have to say anything. As long as it looks like a typical paragraph, it will do. Another sentence or two and it will be long enough. Just one more and it will be perfect! There, that ought to do it.

The words in this paragraph are all filler. Repeated many times, they will give the appearance of a full-length document. On and on the paragraph rambles, drifting further and further into random-sounding

| Pg 2 | Sec 1 | 2/ 3 | At 8" | Ln 43 | Col 11 | 100% | | | NUM | | | |

You can see that using **Ctrl** with ← and → is a good way to skip through a line. The **Ctrl** key has a similar "exaggerating" effect on ↑ and ↓.

8. Press **Home**.

9. Press ↑. The insertion point moves up one line of text.

10. Press **Ctrl**-↑. The insertion point moves to the beginning of the previous paragraph.

Quick&Easy

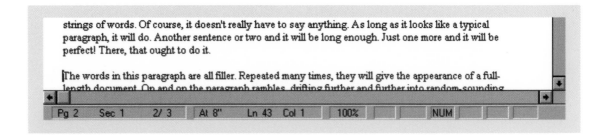

The words in this paragraph are all filler. Repeated many times, they will give the appearance of a full-length document. On and on the paragraph rambles, drifting further and further into random-sounding strings of words. Of course, it doesn't really have to say anything. As long as it looks like a typical paragraph, it will do. Another sentence or two and it will be long enough. Just one more and it will be perfect! There, that ought to do it.

The words in this paragraph are all filler. Repeated many times, they will give the appearance of a full-length document. On and on the paragraph rambles, drifting further and further into random-sounding

Pg 2   Sec 1   2/ 3   At 7"   Ln 37   Col 1   100%   NUM

11. Press ↓. The insertion point moves down one line of text.

12. Press Ctrl-↓. The insertion point moves down to the blank line after this paragraph.

13. Press Ctrl-↓ again. The insertion point moves to the beginning of the next paragraph.

strings of words. Of course, it doesn't really have to say anything. As long as it looks like a typical paragraph, it will do. Another sentence or two and it will be long enough. Just one more and it will be perfect! There, that ought to do it.

The words in this paragraph are all filler. Repeated many times, they will give the appearance of a full-length document. On and on the paragraph rambles, drifting further and further into random-sounding

Pg 2   Sec 1   2/ 3   At 8"   Ln 43   Col 1   100%   NUM

● **Note** In a document like SIESTA, the blank lines between paragraphs each count as separate paragraphs themselves. (This is because Word looks for ↵s to see where a new paragraph starts.)

Finally, I'll show you a few ways to move to another part of the document without moving the insertion point.

Scrolling, Scrolling, Scrolling

There will be times when you'll need to look at another part of your document and then return to exactly where you left off. At such times, you might as well leave the insertion point where it is and just "scroll" to the area you want to look at.

There are three ways to scroll. Try the first way now:

1. Move the mouse pointer to the *vertical* scroll bar, above the scroll box, and click once.

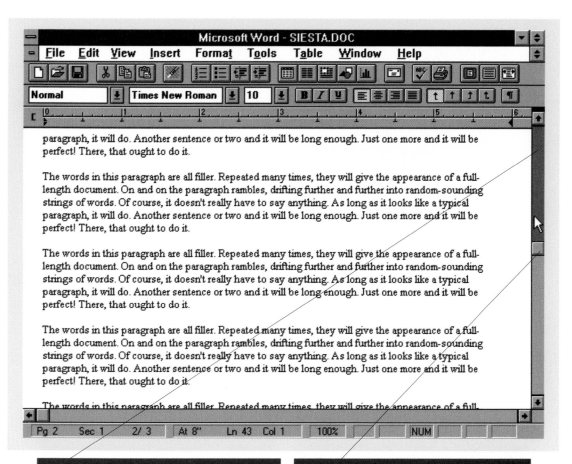

If you have a color screen, the scroll bar darkens when you click it.

The scroll box instantly jumps upward, to give you a sense of where you are in your document.

● **Note** You may never even need to use the *horizontal* scroll bar at the
bottom of the screen. It is for viewing text that is too wide to fit
in the window.

Your view of the text scrolls upward, showing the screenful of
text just above the one you were looking at before. (Notice that
the insertion point is no longer on the screen.) This procedure is
the same one you've already used to scroll through list boxes when
saving or opening documents.

Here is the second way to scroll:

2. Click the downward-pointing scroll arrow at the bottom of
the vertical scroll bar.

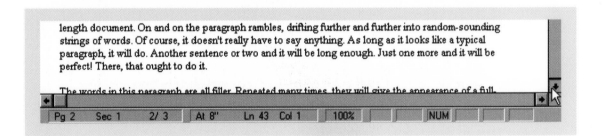

The view scrolls down one line, but not enough to bring the insertion
point back onto the screen (and the scroll box shifts slightly lower).
Use the scroll arrow when you don't want to jump whole screenfuls at
a time.

The final way to scroll allows you the most control:

3. Click the scroll box and drag it to the top of the scroll bar.

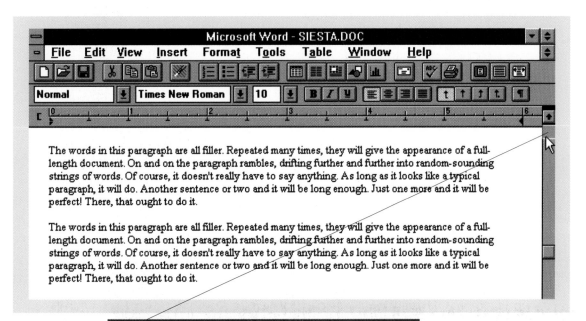

A "ghost image" of the scroll box moves with the arrow until you let go of the mouse button. Then the scroll box itself catches up.

As soon as you release the mouse button, the document scrolls to the top. When you want to see a part of the document somewhere in the middle, drag the scroll box to a position roughly the same fraction of the scroll bar. (For instance, if you want to see a part of the document about a third of the way into it, drag the scroll box about a third of the way down the scroll bar.)

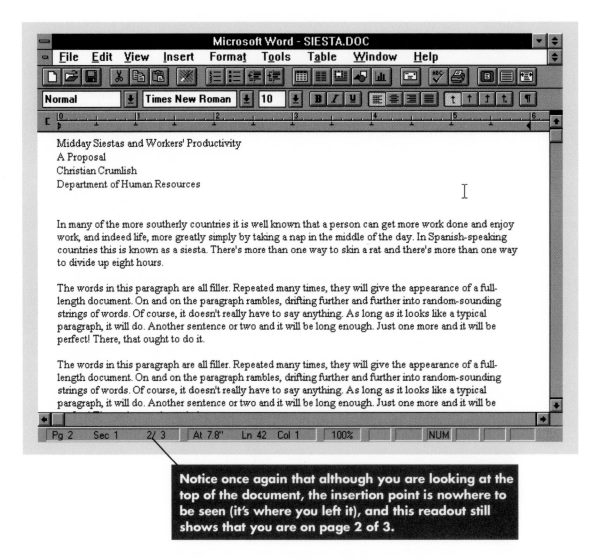

Notice once again that although you are looking at the top of the document, the insertion point is nowhere to be seen (it's where you left it), and this readout still shows that you are on page 2 of 3.

4. Press Ctrl-Home to bring the insertion point to the beginning of the document.

Now you know the ins and outs of finding your way around a long document. You're ready to learn how to improve the appearance of your document.

9

Enhancing Text for Emphasis

So far you've been making plain-vanilla documents. All the text looks the same. Sometimes you'll want to draw attention to a specific word or phrase or even section of your document. Sometimes clear communication requires emphasis. In this lesson I'll show you how to select the text you want to emphasize and then how to make the text **bold**, *italicized,* or <u>underlined</u>. You should have SIESTA.DOC on your screen.

Selecting the Text You Want to Affect

The basic way to select text is to click at one end of the selection and (without letting up the mouse button) drag to the other end of the selection. Try this now:

1. Position the I-beam just before the word *indeed* on the second line of the first paragraph, click, and hold down the mouse button.

2. Drag the I-beam to the end of the word *paragraph* on the first line of the second paragraph and release the mouse button. The selected text is reversed on a black background.

In many of the more southerly countries it is well known that a person can get more work done and enjoy work, and indeed life, more greatly simply by taking a nap in the middle of the day. In Spanish-speaking countries this is known as a siesta. There's more than one way to skin a rat and there's more than one way to divide up eight hours.

The words in this paragraph are all filler. Repeated many times, they will give the appearance of a full-length document. On and on the paragraph rambles, drifting further and further into random-sounding

Notice that the blank line between the paragraphs is also part of the selection.

There are a few slicker shortcuts you might want to know about as well. For instance, you can select a single word.

1. Double-click on the word *indeed.* It is selected.

Department of Human Resources

In many of the more southerly countries it is well known that a person can get more work done and enjoy work, and indeed life, more greatly simply by taking a nap in the middle of the day. In Spanish-speaking countries this is known as a siesta. There's more than one way to skin a rat and there's more than one way to divide up eight hours.

When you select a word, the space immediately after the word is also part of the selection.

You can select an entire sentence.

1. Hold down Ctrl.

2. Click the word *this* on the next line. The sentence is selected.

Department of Human Resources

In many of the more southerly countries it is well known that a person can get more work done and enjoy work, and indeed life, more greatly simply by taking a nap in the middle of the day. In Spanish-speaking countries this is known as a siesta. There's more than one way to skin a rat and there's more than one way to divide up eight hours.

When you select a sentence, the space immediately after the sentence is also part of the selection.

You can also select an entire paragraph:

1. Move the I-beam just to the left of the first word on the second line of the second paragraph (in my case it's the word *length*). The I-beam turns into an arrow pointer.

2. Double-click. The paragraph is selected.

to divide up eight hours.

The words in this paragraph are all filler. Repeated many times, they will give the appearance of a full-length document. On and on the paragraph rambles, drifting further and further into random-sounding strings of words. Of course, it doesn't really have to say anything. As long as it looks like a typical paragraph, it will do. Another sentence or two and it will be long enough. Just one more and it will be perfect! There, that ought to do it.

When you select a paragraph, the invisible ⏎ at the end of the paragraph is also part of the selection.

And, wouldn't you know it, you can select the entire document.

1. Hold down Ctrl.

2. Click in the same place to the left of the word *length*. The document is selected.

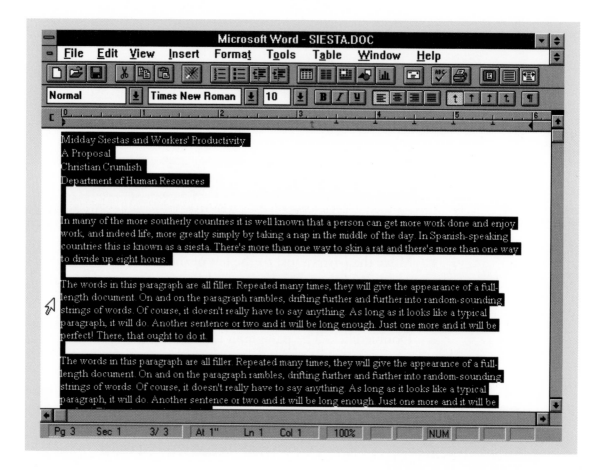

3. Now click somewhere else.

• Note It's too dangerous to keep the whole document selected for very long. It's too easy to delete the whole thing, for example.

Now on to the fun stuff.

To Boldly Go...

Select text, then emphasize—that's the routine. The most common types of emphasis are available on the "ribbon." I don't expect you to remember what that is. It's a stupid name and means nothing to most people. It's the strip below the Toolbar and above the ruler:

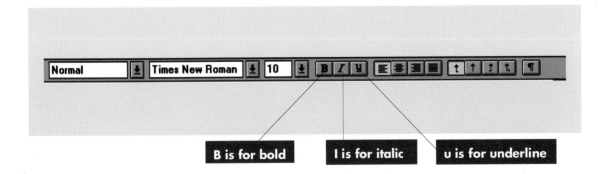

Now, boldface the title of the report.

1. Hold down **Ctrl** and click anywhere in the first line of the report.

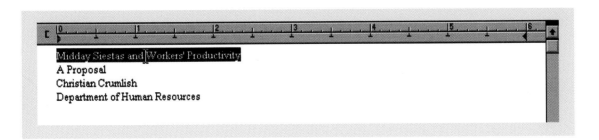

2. Click the Bold button, as shown. The line is boldfaced.

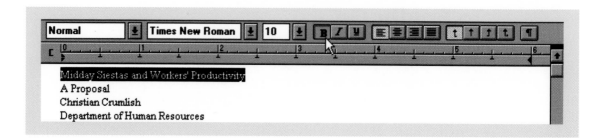

3. Click anywhere to see the bold line more clearly.

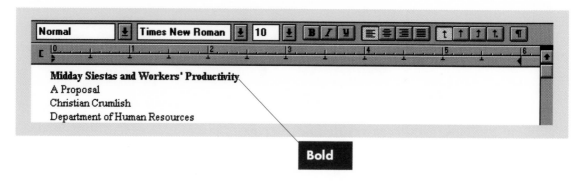

Bold

Now, try out the other two buttons:

4. Select the fourth line, **Department of Human Resources**.

5. Click the Underline button.

6. Select the word *siesta* in the third line of the first paragraph.

7. Click the Italic button.

Midday Siestas and Workers' Productivity
A Proposal
Christian Crumlish
<u>Department of Human Resources</u>

In many of the more southerly countries it is well known that a person can get more work done and enjoy work, and indeed life, more greatly simply by taking a nap in the middle of the day. In Spanish-speaking countries this is known as a *siesta*. There's more than one way to skin a rat and there's more than one way to divide up eight hours.

Underlined   **Italic**

● **Note**   You can combine any and all forms of emphasis. You can make text bold *and* italic. You can underline one bold word in a bold sentence. But wait, there's more.

Emphasis on the Fly

If you know ahead of time that you want to emphasize some text, you can click the appropriate button first, and *then* type the text.

1. Click between the word *anything* and the period that follows it, in the middle of the second paragraph. The insertion point will appear there.

2. Type a space.

3. Click the Italic button.

4. Type **at all**. (Don't type the period—it's one of mine.)

Quick Easy

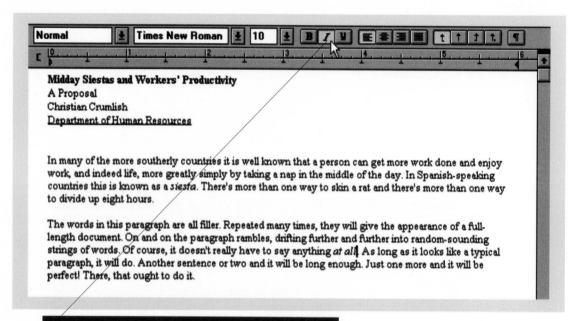

The Italic button remains pressed as you type.

5. Click the Italic button again. It no longer appears to be pressed down.

● Note Get into the habit of unpressing buttons when you are finished using them. It's sometimes inconvenient when you forget to.

You can remove emphasis just as easily. If you change your mind or want to remove emphasis you've added by mistake, just select the text and click the button so it's *not* pressed down. The emphasis will be removed.

That's all you need to know about emphasis. There *are* other ways to improve the appearance of your words. In the next lesson, I'll show you how to change the size and the style of text.

10

Changing Font and Size

As I mentioned at the end of the previous lesson, there are still other ways to vary or improve the appearance of your text. We'll continue to use the SIESTA report as a guinea pig as I show you how to change two things: font and size. Font means type style; size you know.

Use Different Fonts for Different Occasions

Some fonts are formal and look authoritative. Others are more casual and relaxed. Some are easier to read than others. Some make good, attention-grabbing headlines. Word (or really Windows) comes with a basic set of fonts, so you are provided with some variety. Look at the ribbon again. The only font you've probably used so far is called Times New Roman. Do you see it? You're about to select some text and change its font.

1. Select the first line of the report title.

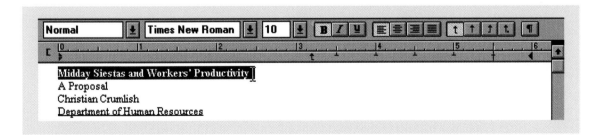

Quick Easy

2. Click the down arrow on the ribbon to the right of the
words **Times New Roman**. It brings down a list of available
fonts; the current one is highlighted.

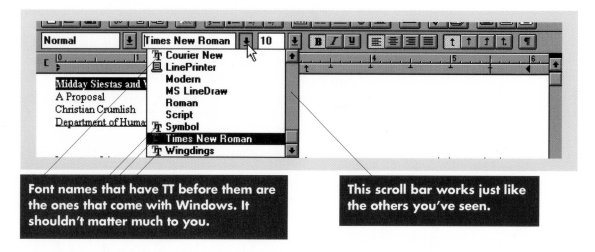

**Font names that have TT before them are
the ones that come with Windows. It
shouldn't matter much to you.**

**This scroll bar works just like
the others you've seen.**

3. Click in the scroll bar above the scroll box. You're taken to
the top of the font list.

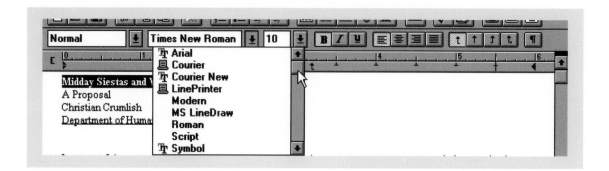

4. Click on the word **Arial** at the top of the list, as shown. The list box disappears as soon as you release the mouse button.

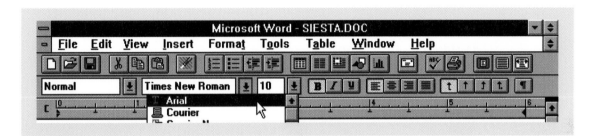

5. Click anywhere to see the change more clearly.

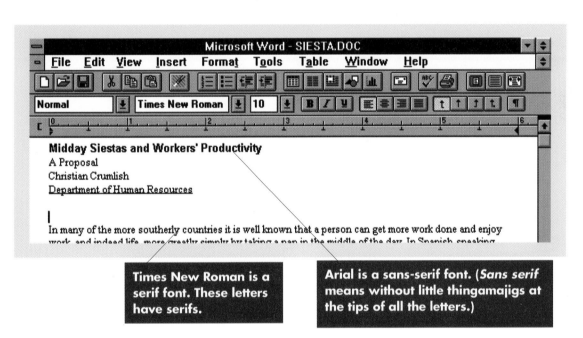

Times New Roman is a serif font. These letters have serifs.

Arial is a sans-serif font. (*Sans serif* means without little thingamajigs at the tips of all the letters.)

It's that easy to change fonts. Experiment sometime with the fonts you have available, just so you know what you've got. You can also change to a new font and *then* type your text in that font.

Now let's try some different sizes.

One Size Doesn't Fit All

Changing the size of your text is as easy as changing the font. Follow these instructions to make the report's title text bigger. The first line is the title itself, so it needs to be the largest.

1. Select the title of the report.

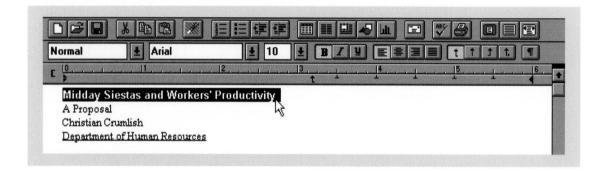

2. Click the down arrow on the ribbon to the right of the number **10**. A drop-down list box appears.

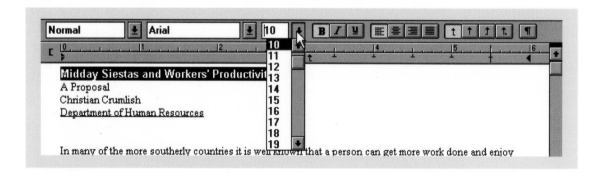

● Note Text size is measured in units called "points." Everything you've typed so far has been 10-point text. Typewriters usually make letters between 10 and 12 points high (about one-sixth of an inch).

You don't want to make the title *too* big.

3. Click **14**, as shown:

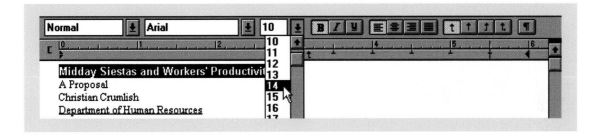

4. Click anywhere to see the result.

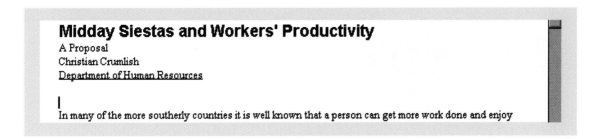

Now the next three lines look too small. Set their point size to 12.

5. Select the next three lines.

6. Pull down the size list again.

7. Click **12**.

8. Click somewhere else.

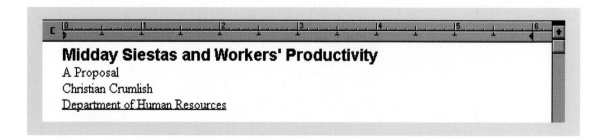

There, now doesn't that look imposing and authoritative? Just as with fonts and many other Word features, you can always set a new size and then type the text you want in that size.

In the next lesson, I'll show you how to center text or otherwise change its alignment.

Positioning Text on the Page

Look at your document. Notice how all the words line up along the left edge? Also, notice how they're uneven at the right edge? This is called "left alignment," or "ragged right." It's the way typewritten words look. Maybe you like the way it looks just fine. Most of the time it will do. But there are a few other options. Let's try some of them now with the SIESTA report.

Taking Center Stage

Turn your attention once again to the ribbon. To the right of the Bold, Italic, and Underline buttons is a set of four buttons with lines on them, each representing a different alignment option. The first one is pressed down:

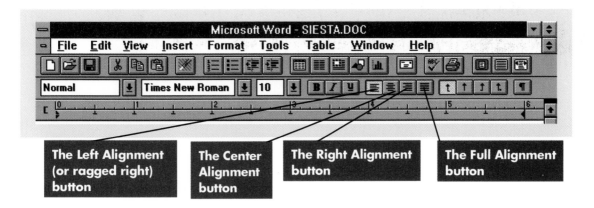

The Left Alignment (or ragged right) button

The Center Alignment button

The Right Alignment button

The Full Alignment button

Center the title and subtitle:

1. Select the first two lines.

2. Click the Center Alignment button, as shown:

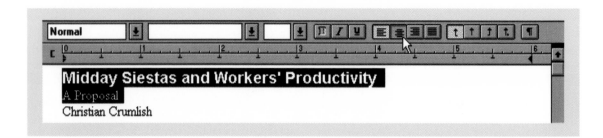

3. Click anywhere. Your title and subtitle should look like this:

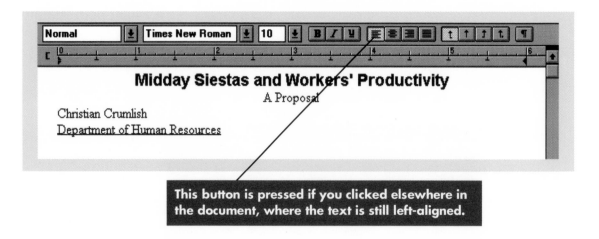

This button is pressed if you clicked elsewhere in the document, where the text is still left-aligned.

Let's give the title a little breathing room:

4. Click just to the left of the report author's name, so the insertion point is before the first letter.

Note If you click too far to the left, you'll select the whole line. Just click again until you get it right.

5. Press ↵.

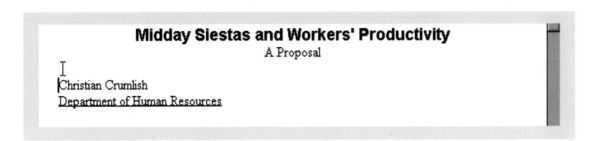

On the Right Side

Now let's move the name and department to the right:

1. Select the name and the underlined department name.

2. Click the Right Alignment button, as shown:

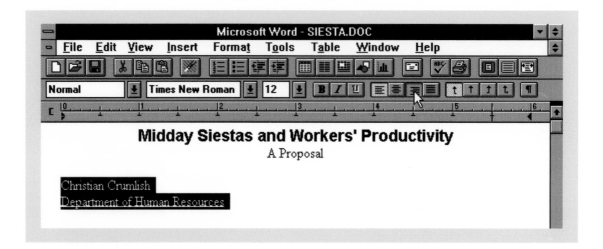

3. Click somewhere else. Your screen should look like this:

What could be easier?

Justification in Time

There's one other alignment button you haven't yet seen in action. It aligns the text at the left *and* the right. How does it do this? Well, it spaces out the words as necessary so that all lines are the same length (except the last lines of paragraphs). Most normal books have this sort of alignment, which is also called *full justification.* It makes text look more formal, more "published." Although it may not be appropriate for something simple like a memo, it's just the thing for a report. (Also, the words below the name will line up with it on the right edge.) So let's try it on the body text.

1. Place the I-beam anywhere in the first paragraph and click. The insertion point should appear where you clicked.

Department of Human Resources

In many of the more southerly countries it is well known that a person can get more work done and enjoy work, and indeed life, more greatly simply by taking a nap in the middle of the day. In Spanish-speaking countries this is known as a *siesta.* There's more than one way to skin a rat and there's more than one way to divide up eight hours.

2. Click the Full Alignment button, as shown:

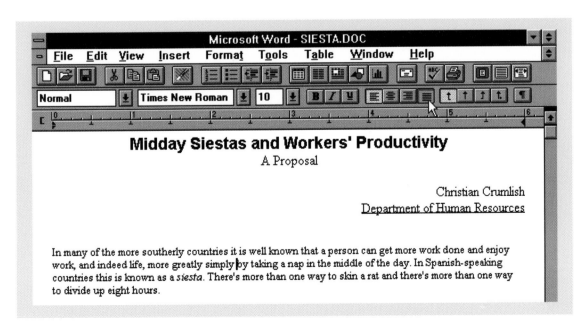

Quick & Easy

The paragraph is now fully justified:

In many of the more southerly countries it is well known that a person can get more work done and enjoy work, and indeed life, more greatly simply by taking a nap in the middle of the day. In Spanish-speaking countries this is known as a *siesta*. There's more than one way to skin a rat and there's more than one way to divide up eight hours.

The words in this paragraph are all filler. Repeated many times, they will give the appearance of a full-length document. On and on the paragraph rambles, drifting farther and further into random-sounding strings of words. Of course, it doesn't really have to say anything *at all*. As long as it looks like a typical paragraph, it will do. Another sentence or two and it will be long enough. Just one more and it will be perfect! There, that ought to do it.

The first paragraph is now fully justified.

The next paragraph is still left-justified (as are all the rest).

● Note When you centered the title lines, you first selected them both. I had you do this because each one ends with a ↵, and Word considers each to be a separate paragraph. If you just place the insertion point somewhere *in* a paragraph, and then set the alignment, just that paragraph is realigned. To affect more than one paragraph at a time, you must make a selection that includes text in both or all of the paragraphs you mean to affect.

The easiest way to give the rest of the document full alignment is to select all the paragraphs (or to make a selection that starts *anywhere* in the first paragraph and ends anywhere in the last one). To do this, I'll show you a new way to select text.

1. Place the I-beam anywhere in the second paragraph and click.

2. Drag the scroll box to the bottom of the scroll bar. You can now see the end of the report.

3. Hold down **Shift** and click anywhere in the last paragraph. You see the end of a selection that stretches back to the first page of the report.

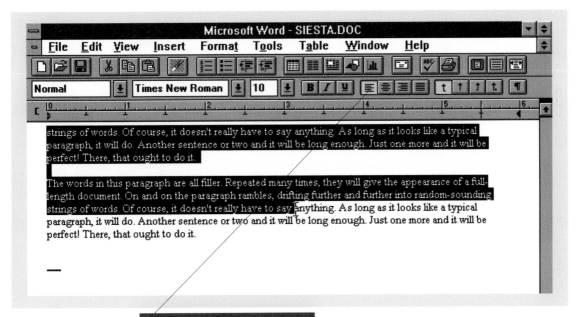

This button tells you that these paragraphs are still left-aligned.

• Note This method of clicking at one end of a selection and then Shift-clicking at the other is a good way of selecting text that doesn't all fit on the screen at once.

4. Click the Full Alignment button. The rest of the report is now fully justified.

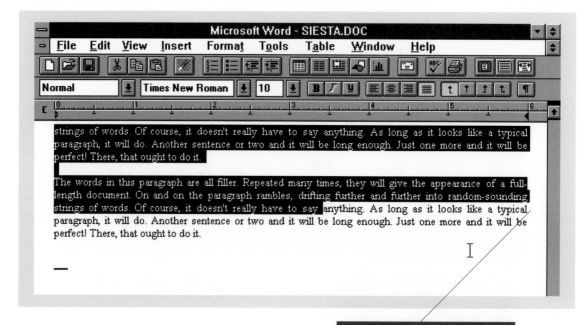

The entire final paragraph
is fully justified, not just
the selected part.

5. Press **Ctrl-Home** to get back to the beginning of the report.

So now you know how to put the words wherever you want them on
the page.

12

Paragraph Indents the Quick Way

By now you may realize that Word separates the two jobs of typing and formatting. When you are trying to write something, you should not have to be thinking about how it's going to look. You just want to type in your words. Later, you can go back and fix up their appearance. In the last lesson, I showed you how to change paragraph alignment. In this lesson and the next few, I'll show you other easy paragraph formatting tricks.

Indents in the Wink of an Eye

In both sample documents I've asked you to type, each paragraph begins without an indent. Each one is flush with the left margin. This is the best way to type even if you'd like your paragraphs to start with an indent. There's no point in typing spaces or tabs before the first word of *every* paragraph. In some cases that will even end up inconveniencing you.

Fortunately, there is a way to indent one or all of your paragraphs after you've finished typing them. I'll show you how to do this now.

To indent the paragraphs in your SIESTA report, just do this:

1. Make a selection that starts in the first paragraph of the document (don't include the title or name) and ends anywhere in the last.

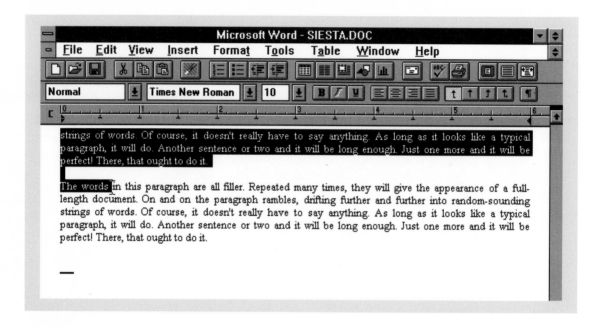

• Note This type of selection is explained in Lesson 11.

Now, look at the ruler. Just below the **0** at the left end is a split triangle pointing to the right. The only thing you really need to know about is the *top half* of that triangle. Its position indicates the paragraph indent (currently zero inches—meaning no indent).

2. Click the indent marker and drag it to the halfway point between the **0** and **1**, as shown:

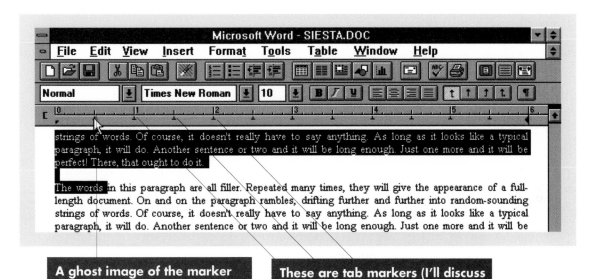

A ghost image of the marker slides with you as you drag the pointer into place.

These are tab markers (I'll discuss them in Lesson 14).

The last paragraph (which you can see) and all the other paragraphs (which you can't) are indented $1/2$ inch.

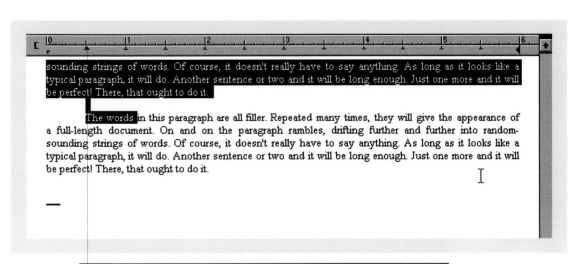

The indent marker is at the half-inch mark (it looks a little funny because it's sharing the space with a tab marker).

3. Press Ctrl-Home to see the beginning of the report.

The indent marker is back at zero because the insertion point is at the beginning of the title, which you didn't indent.

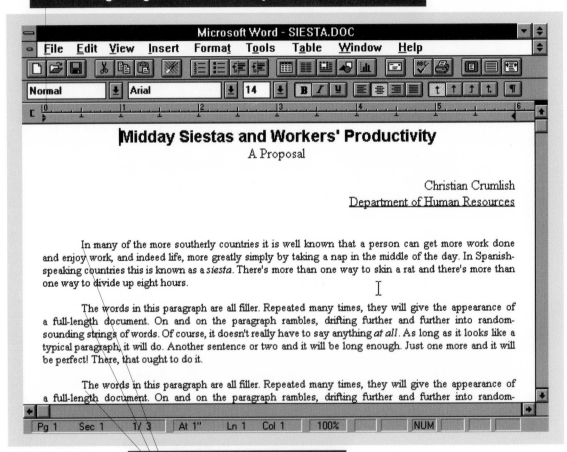

All the paragraphs are indented.

That's all you need to know.

● **Note** As with all the formatting I've discussed, you can set a paragraph indent just *before* you type a paragraph. Then all the following paragraphs you type will be indented as well. But there's no real need to plan ahead like that.

13

5 MINUTES

Double Spacing—the Editor's Friend

Most long documents will go through a few drafts before you're done with them. Even in this computer age, most people like to print things out on paper to read them over and see how they look on the page. If others are going to look at something you've written and offer suggestions or advice, they'll appreciate it if your document is double-spaced. For that matter, you'll like it too if you plan to reread your work and scribble changes or comments to yourself. You may even want your final documents double-spaced at times. I double-space these lessons when I submit them to my editor. (He makes me!)

When Single Spacing Just Isn't Enough

By now you know the drill. Changing line spacing is the kind of thing you want to do to all your paragraphs at once. As with all the formatting I've discussed, you can choose double spacing before you type your paragraphs, but then fewer lines will fit on the screen and you won't be able to see as much of your work as you go. So my advice is to wait till you're done typing. Of course, that's always my advice.

From your SIESTA report, follow these steps:

1. Select text from the first paragraph to the last.

● Note This type of selection is explained in Lesson 11.

2. Pull down the Format menu and select Paragraph, as shown:

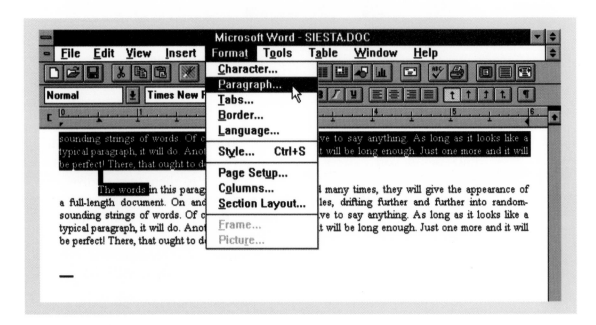

You'll see this dialog box:

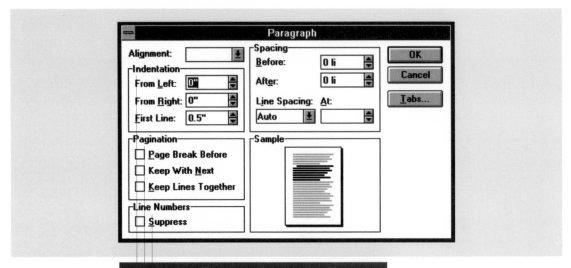

You'll be glad to know you can ignore most of what you see in this dialog box.

3. In the **Spacing** area, click the arrow to the right of the word **Auto**, as shown:

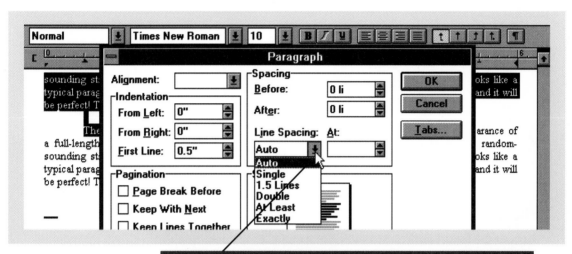

Although you started out with "Auto" spacing, there isn't much difference worth explaining between that and Single.

4. Click Double.

In the Sample area, you are shown how double spacing looks in a sample paragraph.

5. Click OK.

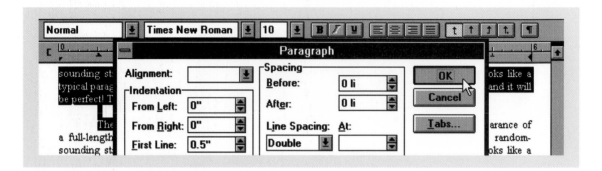

The paragraphs are now double-spaced.

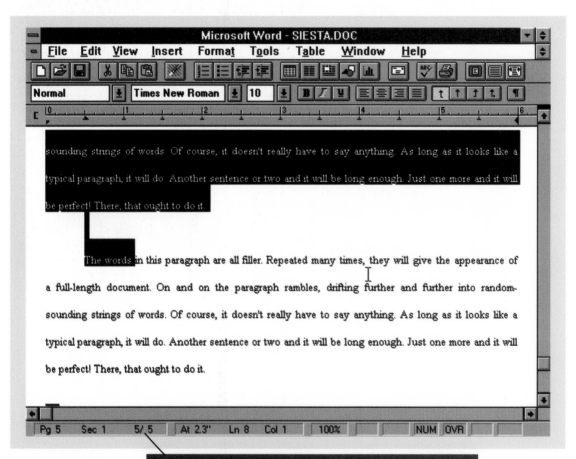

The document is now five pages long because of the double spacing.

6. Press **Ctrl-Home** to return to the top of the document.

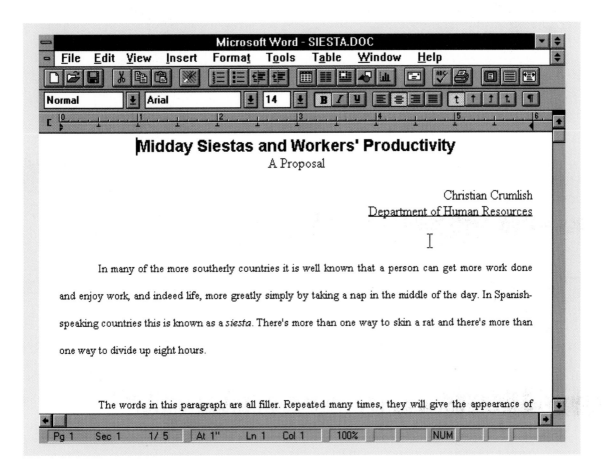

If you need to change your spacing back, go through the same steps—select Paragraph on the Format menu—and then choose Auto again in the Line Spacing list box.

Setting Your Own Tabs

14

If you want to line up information in columns, one easy way to do that is with tabs. In the first document you typed, the memo, tabs lined up the names, date, and subject. (Some people use tabs to indent the beginnings of paragraphs, but I've already shown you a better way to do that.) In this lesson, you'll use the tabs Word provides and then see how to set your own when you need to.

Word's Half-Inch Tabs

When you press Tab, the insertion point moves to the next "tab stop," the next place where a tab has been set. Word starts you off with a tab stop every half inch. These can be quite useful, as you'll see:

1. Click the New button (the leftmost one on the Toolbar) to start a new document.

2. Type the following:

1 `Tab` 1 `Tab` 2 `Tab` 3 `Tab` 5 `↵`
8 `Tab` 13 `Tab` 21 `Tab` 34 `Tab` 55 `↵`
89 `Tab` 144 `Tab` 233 `Tab` 377 `Tab` 610 `↵`

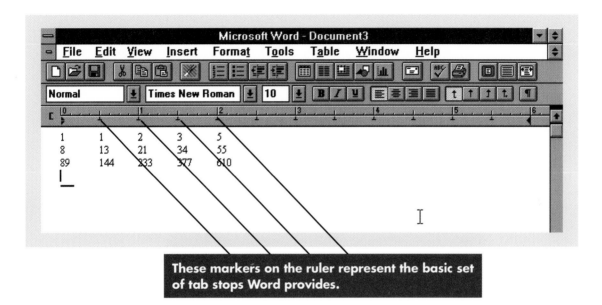

These markers on the ruler represent the basic set of tab stops Word provides.

See how the numbers line up neatly?

When You Need to Set Your Own Tabs

Sometimes, however, the words you're trying to line up won't fall neatly into half-inch columns. Try creating this list to see what I mean:

1. Hit ↵ twice.

2. Click the Bold button.

3. Type

Name [Tab] Title [Tab] Years with Firm [↵]

4. Click the Bold button again.

5. Type the following:

Jane Doe [Tab] Chair and CEO [Tab] 13 [↵]

Jaime Martinez [Tab] President and CFO [Tab] 8 [↵]

Jasper J. Carruthers III [Tab] Executive Vice President [Tab] 3 [↵]

Sandy Ozark [Tab] Chief Bottle-Washer [Tab] 16 [↵]

Your screen should look something like this:

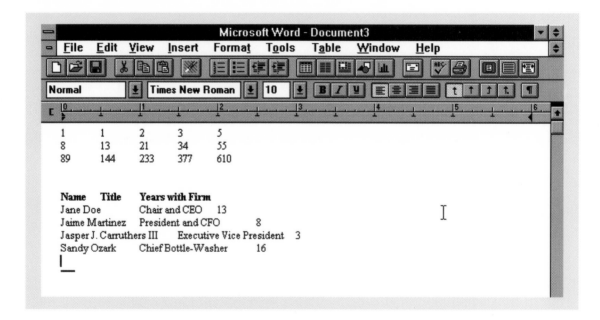

As you can see, the different words vary greatly in length, so they don't line up. You need to set specific tabs that work for this particular list.

6. Select the entire list.

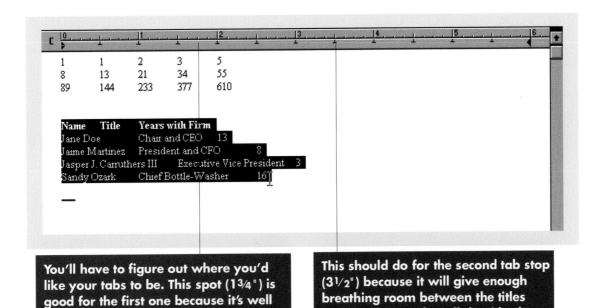

You'll have to figure out where you'd like your tabs to be. This spot (1¾") is good for the first one because it's well past the longest of the names.

This should do for the second tab stop (3½") because it will give enough breathing room between the titles and the years, after all the titles have slid over.

7. Click on the ruler at the 1¾-inch mark.

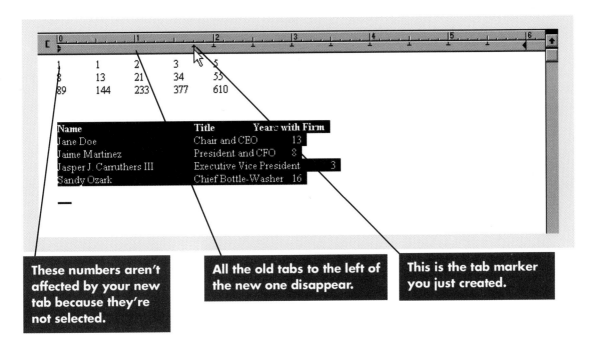

These numbers aren't affected by your new tab because they're not selected.

All the old tabs to the left of the new one disappear.

This is the tab marker you just created.

8. Click on the ruler at the 3½-inch mark.

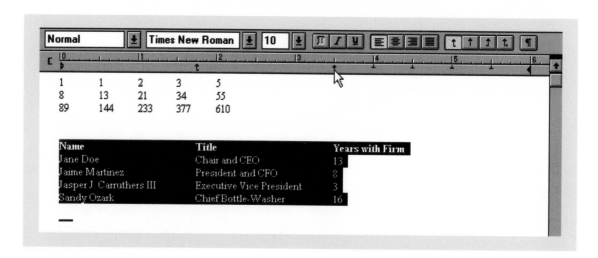

But you don't have to pinpoint the perfect locations for your tabs
ahead of time. After you've placed them, you can move them around
just by dragging (keep the text selected until you're satisfied).

9. Click the first tab marker you set and drag it to about
1⅝ inches.

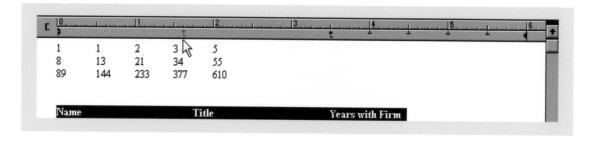

The words adjust as soon as you release the mouse button.

● Note   If you ever change your mind about the tabs you've set, just click on the markers and drag them off the ruler; the old, built-in tabs will reappear.

Since I only had you create this document to play around with tabs a little, you might as well get rid of it now:

1. Pull down the <u>F</u>ile menu and select <u>C</u>lose.

2. When Word asks you if you want to save the changes, click <u>N</u>o.

In the next couple of lessons, you'll learn about things you can do to the whole page.

Using Margins to Control the Look of the Page

15

In the last few lessons, you've learned how to do formatting that affects paragraphs. In this lesson and the next few, I'll show you some things you can do to affect the look of the page. The margins (top and bottom, left and right) control where the words appear on the page. I'll show you how to change the margins and why you might want to.

Setting All the Margins at Once

Word starts you off with 1-inch margins at the top and bottom of your page, and 1¼ -inch margins on the left and right sides. You may find these margins, which are fairly standard, to be perfectly acceptable. But you may also want to change them. You may want to make your document seem longer, or shorter. You may want to make it easier to read. The Times Roman font can be sort of spindly and hard on the eyes, so let's set left and right margins to make a shorter line length, and increase the top and bottom margins to make a shorter page of text.

1. If you don't currently have SIESTA on the screen, switch to it or open it.

2. Pull down the File menu and select Print Preview, as shown:

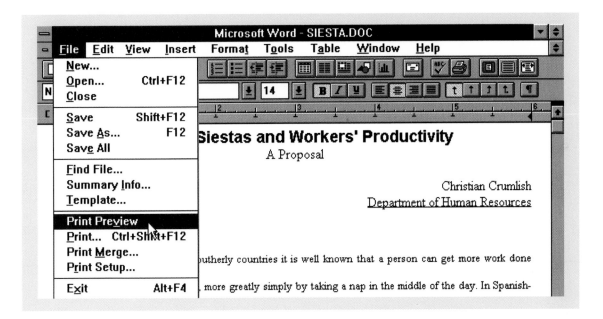

You'll see a view of the entire first page of the document, with the words too small to read.

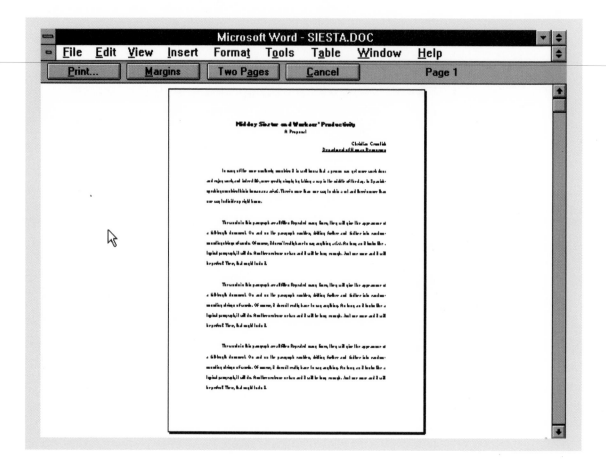

3. Click the Margins button, as shown:

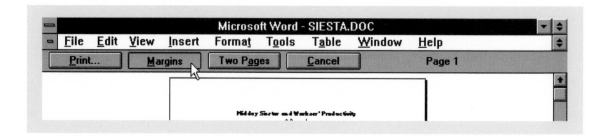

Lines appear on the page. They represent the current margins.

Microsoft Word - SIESTA.DOC

| File | Edit | View | Insert | Format | Tools | Table | Window | Help |

| Print... | Margins | Two Pages | Cancel | Page 1 |

Midday Siesta and Workers' Productivity
A Proposal

Christian Crosslink
Department of Human Resources

**These four black squares are "handles."
You click on them and drag the margins
into position.**

4. Click on the top-margin "handle" and hold down the
mouse button.

Quick & Easy

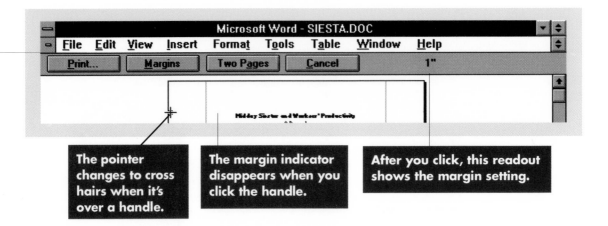

The pointer changes to cross hairs when it's over a handle.

The margin indicator disappears when you click the handle.

After you click, this readout shows the margin setting.

5. Watching the margin readout, drag the margin to the 1.5 " position.

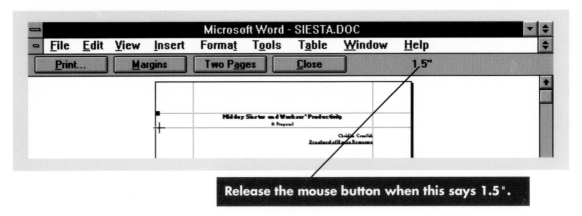

Release the mouse button when this says 1.5 ".

6. After releasing the mouse button, click outside the edges of the page and the text on the screen readjusts to fit the new margin.

● Note Any changes you make to the margins affect all the pages of your document—not just the one you see on the Print Preview screen.

7. Now click the left-margin handle and drag it to create a 2-inch left margin.

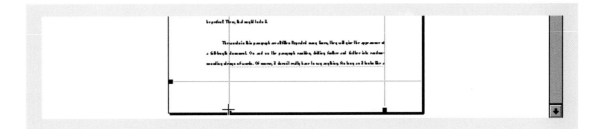

8. Drag the right-margin handle to create a 1½-inch right margin.

9. Click outside the page again. The page looks different now, doesn't it?

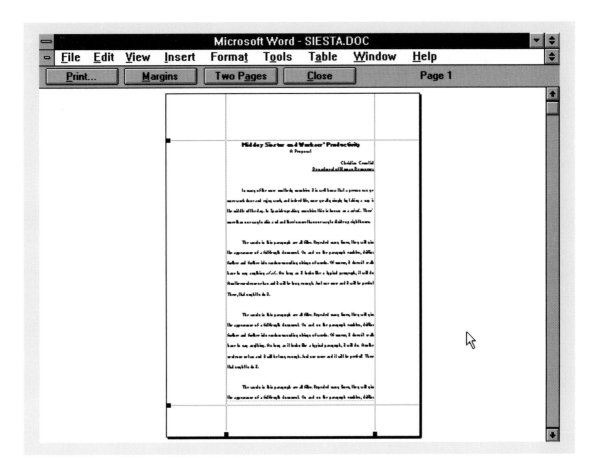

10. Click <u>C</u>lose, as shown:

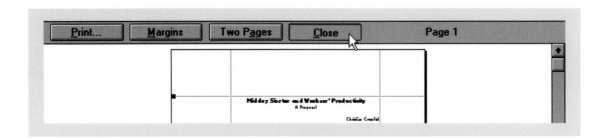

It's one thing to see how the entire page will look. It's another to see the effects of your margin changes when you return to the usual view of your document. Maybe we made the lines a little short. You can fix that without returning to Print Preview.

Changing Left and Right Margins on the Ruler

The line length *does* look a little short now. Remember, you made the left margin 2 inches wide. Here's how to ease it back out a little by using just the ruler.

1. Click the bracket symbol ([) at the left end of the ruler, as shown:

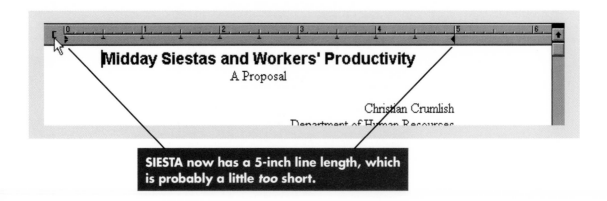

SIESTA now has a 5-inch line length, which is probably a little *too* short.

The indent and tab markers immediately disappear from beneath the tick marks on the ruler and brackets appear, indicating the margins. The numbers on the ruler also change to show the distances from the left edge of the page instead of from the left margin of the document.

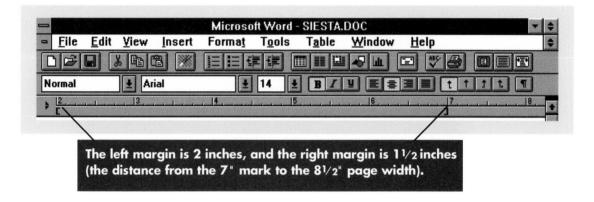

The left margin is 2 inches, and the right margin is 1½ inches (the distance from the 7" mark to the 8½" page width).

Normally, if you want to move a margin, you just click on the bracket and drag it to its new location. In this case, however, you want to drag the bracket to the *left,* to a part of the ruler that's not visible right now, so you have to fake to the right first. Here's how you do it:

2. Click the left bracket and drag it a little ways to the right (don't release the mouse button).

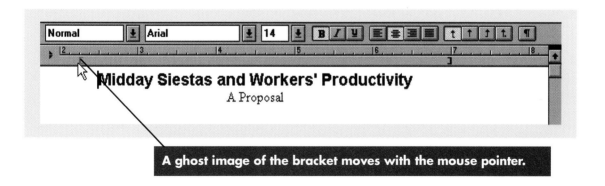

A ghost image of the bracket moves with the mouse pointer.

3. Now, drag the bracket to the left. When you pass the most recent left margin position, the text will jump to the right and more of the ruler will come into view. Move the bracket to the $1\frac{1}{2}$-inch mark.

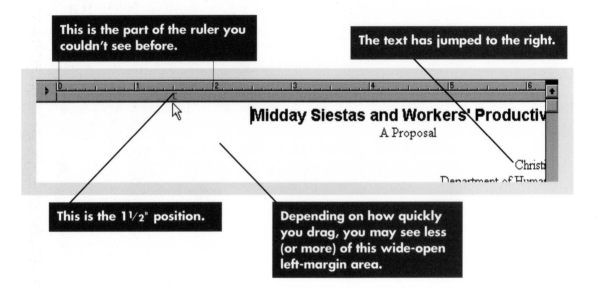

This is the part of the ruler you couldn't see before.

The text has jumped to the right.

Midday Siestas and Workers' Productiv

A Proposal

This is the 1½" position.

Depending on how quickly you drag, you may see less (or more) of this wide-open left-margin area.

4. Release the mouse button. The words immediately adjust to the new margin (and the ruler may shift again).

The ruler has shifted farther to the right (for no real reason).

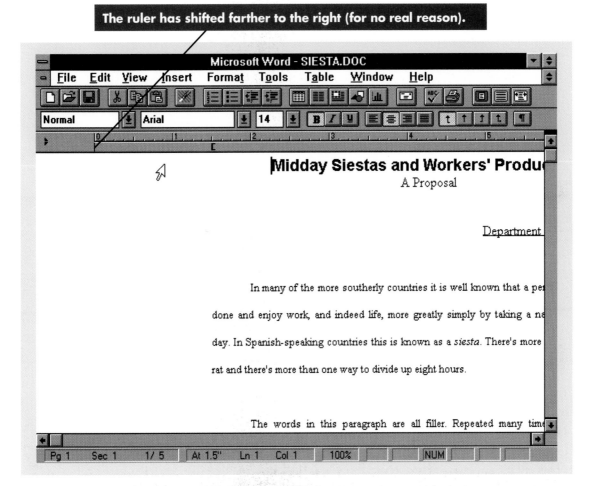

Of course, you will want to get your text back fully on the screen.

5. Click the scroll box on the horizontal scroll bar, drag it a wee bit to the right, and then drag it immediately back all the way to the left. Then release it.

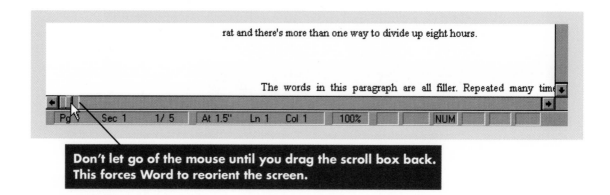

rat and there's more than one way to divide up eight hours.

The words in this paragraph are all filler. Repeated many time

| Pg | Sec 1 | 1/ 5 | At 1.5" | Ln 1 | Col 1 | 100% | NUM | |

**Don't let go of the mouse until you drag the scroll box back.
This forces Word to reorient the screen.**

Again you see the results of your margin change immediately. The advantage of the ruler method is that you can do it and keep typing without missing a beat. One drawback is that you can't change top and bottom margins with the ruler.

Now, take the ruler out of its margin mode and you'll be done.

6. Click the indent symbol at the left end of the ruler. The indent and tab markers reappear.

In the next lesson, I'll show you how to set up a header or footer to appear on every page.

Numbering Your Pages in a Flash

Now that I've got you thinking about how your pages will look, I'll move on to some other ways you can enhance the appearance of your documents. For instance, SIESTA is five pages long, right? How did you know that? Well, Word tells you—it shows up on the bottom of the screen. But what about your readers? They'd appreciate seeing page numbers. In this lesson I'll show you a very easy, straightforward way to set up automatic page numbering.

Inserting Page Numbers with No Muss, No Fuss

The best thing about doing your page numbering with Word is that you only have to do it once. You set up the numbers and then Word makes sure they're accurate. If you make changes to your document and it gets longer or shorter, Word renumbers the pages. Here's what you do:

1. Pull down the Insert menu and select Page Numbers, as shown:

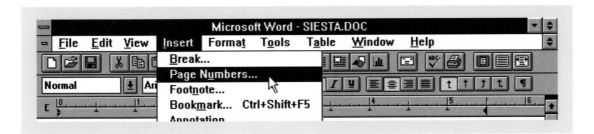

This dialog box appears:

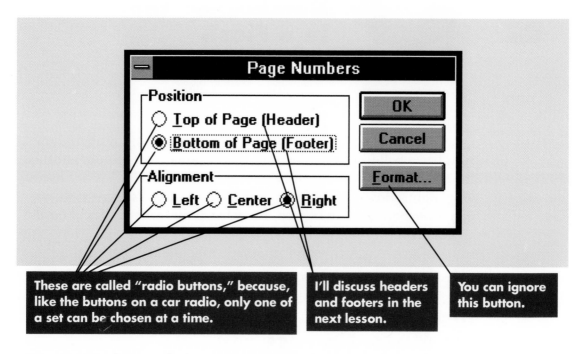

These are called "radio buttons," because, like the buttons on a car radio, only one of a set can be chosen at a time.

I'll discuss headers and footers in the next lesson.

You can ignore this button.

You are given choices of where you want the page numbers to appear: top or bottom, left, center, or right. The bottom of the page is fine, but how about putting the page numbers in the center?

2. Click Center, as shown:

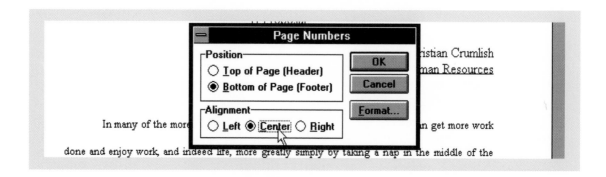

3. Click OK.

That's all there is to it.

> **● Note** If you set up page numbers this way, numbering starts on the second page of your document (because many people prefer it that way). Page 1 is unnumbered, a 2 appears on page 2, and so on. If you prefer to have numbering start on the first page, you'll need to set up a header or footer, as you'll see in Lesson 17.

How to See Your New Page Numbers

Of course, you only have my word to go on that you've got page numbers now. If you look around, you won't see them.

1. Make sure you're at the top of SIESTA. Press PageDown five times (until you can see the second page break, which separates page 2 from page 3).

The insertion point is in roughly the same position it was in on the first page.

There is no page number in sight.

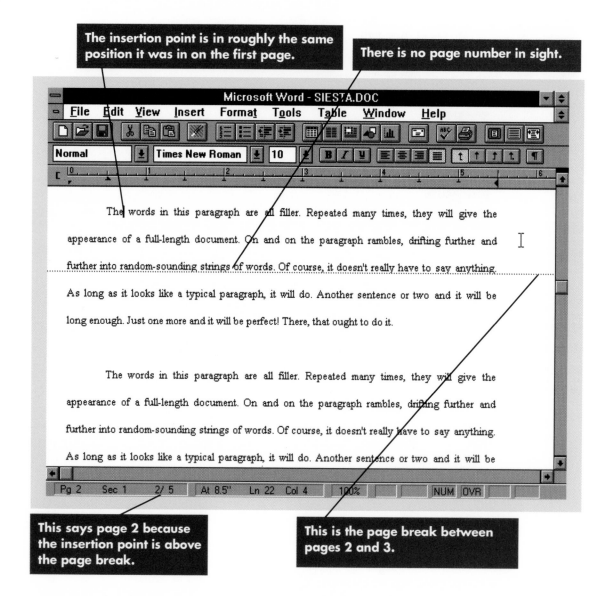

This says page 2 because the insertion point is above the page break.

This is the page break between pages 2 and 3.

This page is where the first page number is supposed to be. One way to verify that it's there is to choose "page layout" view, which allows you to see the entire page with everything on it. (In the normal view you don't see any repeating stuff, like page numbers.)

2. Pull down the <u>V</u>iew menu and select <u>P</u>age Layout, as shown:

The view changes:

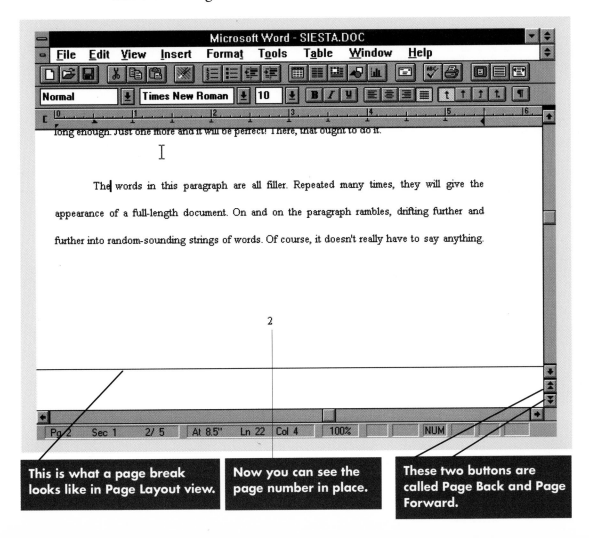

This is what a page break looks like in Page Layout view.

Now you can see the page number in place.

These two buttons are called Page Back and Page Forward.

3. Click the Page Forward button, as shown:

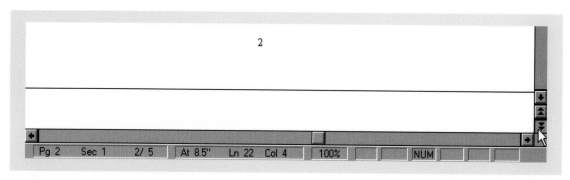

You jump to the bottom of page 3.

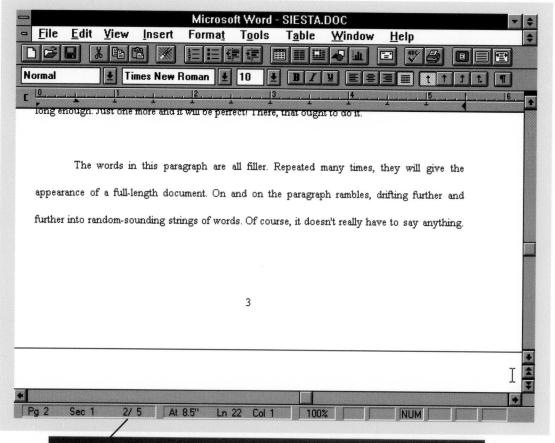

Your view has changed but the insertion point is still where you left it, at the end of page 2.

Most of the time when you're working, though, you'll appreciate *not* seeing page numbers, headings, etc.

4. Pull down the <u>V</u>iew menu and select <u>N</u>ormal, as shown:

5. Press Ctrl-Home.

In the next lesson, I'll show you how to set up headers and footers, which work very much the same way page numbers do.

5 MINUTES

Straightforward Headers and Footers

17

As long as you want only a page number to show up on each page (after the first), you'll be fine using what you learned in the previous lesson. If you want something different—numbers that start on the first page, your name or a title on every page, the date of the current draft—you've got to set up a header or a footer. (A header is something that appears at the top—the "head"—of every page. A footer appears at the bottom—the "foot.") But don't worry. It's still pretty easy.

You Have to View Them to Set Them Up

The first step in setting up a header or a footer is to view the space where it's going to be. Start at the top of your SIESTA report.

1. Pull down the <u>V</u>iew menu and select <u>H</u>eader/Footer, as shown:

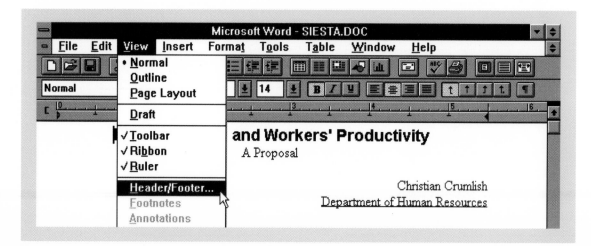

You'll see this dialog box:

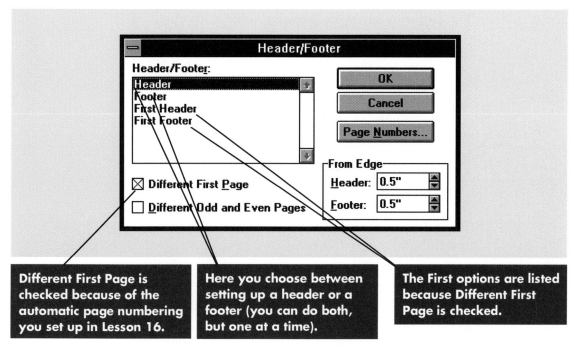

Different First Page is checked because of the automatic page numbering you set up in Lesson 16.

Here you choose between setting up a header or a footer (you can do both, but one at a time).

The First options are listed because Different First Page is checked.

● **Note** This dialog box would look different if you had never set up page numbers in the first place. Different First Page would not be checked, and there would be only two options: Header and Footer.

2. Click Different First Page to unselect it. Two of the options in the box disappear.

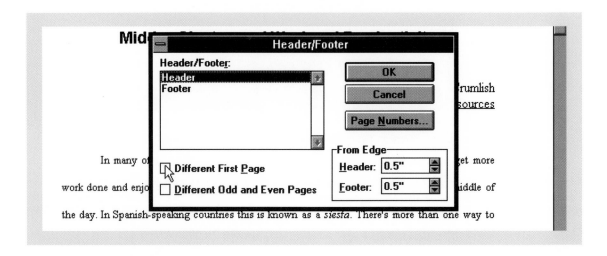

3. Select Footer.

4. Click OK.

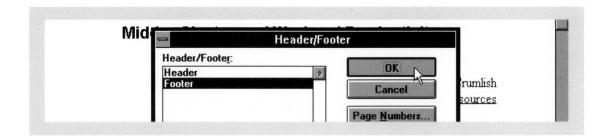

A special area called a "pane" opens up at the bottom of the screen.

● Note A pane is just a special area on the screen for making things like footers and notes. You can do most normal typing and word processing in them.

This is the Page Number button. You click it to insert a page number.

This is the Date button. You click it to insert the current date.

This is the Time button. You click it to insert the current time (for very exact people only!).

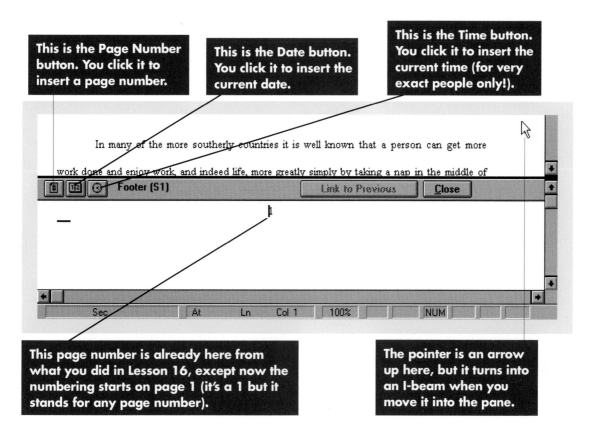

This page number is already here from what you did in Lesson 16, except now the numbering starts on page 1 (it's a 1 but it stands for any page number).

The pointer is an arrow up here, but it turns into an I-beam when you move it into the pane.

In a footer (or header) you can put information in any of three preset positions—left, middle, or right—just by using the Tab key. Let's put the author's name at the left, the current date in the middle, and the page number at the right.

5. Type the author's name and press Tab.

6. Click the Date button, as shown:

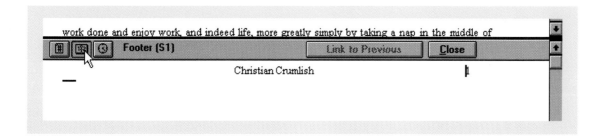

● Note The name and date are not in the proper position yet. This is because the page number was already there in the middle when you started. You'll fix that next.

7. Press **Tab**. The name and the current date shift to the left.

8. Click <u>C</u>lose, as shown:

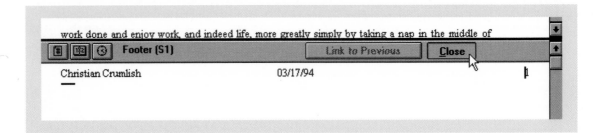

And that's all there is to setting up a footer. The steps are exactly the same for a header (except you have to select Header, of course, in the Header/Footer dialog box). If you want to change a header or footer later, you just view them again and then make changes as you would in a regular document.

18

Making a Title Page

5 MINUTES

If you are writing a formal document, you may want it to have a title page. To give it one, you have to insert a special page break after the title information so that the actual text of the document starts on the second page. You also have to make any header or footer skip the first page. I'll show you how.

Forcing Word to Start a New Page

Normally, you don't have to tell Word when to start a new page. You just keep typing and when one page is full, a new one starts. In some ways this is similar to word wrap. You type a paragraph and Word breaks the lines where they fit. At any point you can press ↵ and force Word to start a new line. So it shouldn't be too hard to remember that pressing Ctrl-↵ starts a new page. Try it now with SIESTA:

1. Position the insertion point just before the word *In* at the beginning of the first paragraph.

2. Press Ctrl-↵. A dotted line appears.

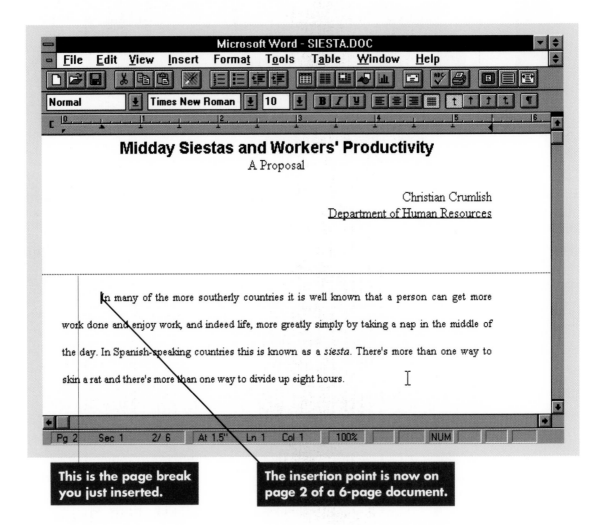

This is the page break you just inserted.

The insertion point is now on page 2 of a 6-page document.

Now the title info is on a page by itself. Of course, it's at the very top of the page, so let's bring it down closer to the middle.

3. Press Ctrl-Home.

4. Press ↵ twelve times.

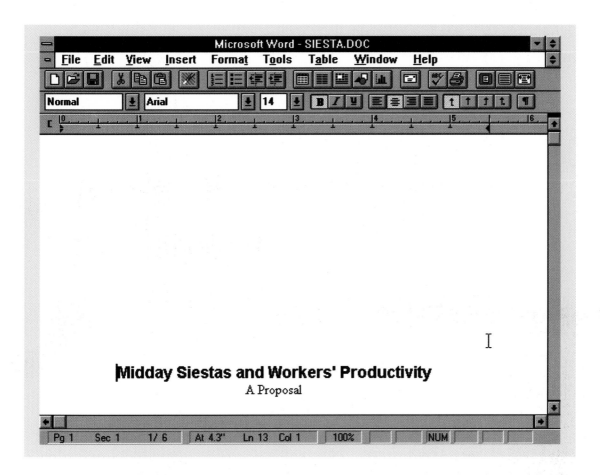

• Note Unfortunately, there's no easy way to center text on a page in Word. (It *is* possible, but it's not worth going into.) The easiest approach, therefore, is to hit ↵ a bunch of times until the words are more or less in the middle of the page.

Now, use Print Preview to see the whole page.

5. Pull down the File menu and select Print Preview. You'll see your title page in full.

Quick&Easy

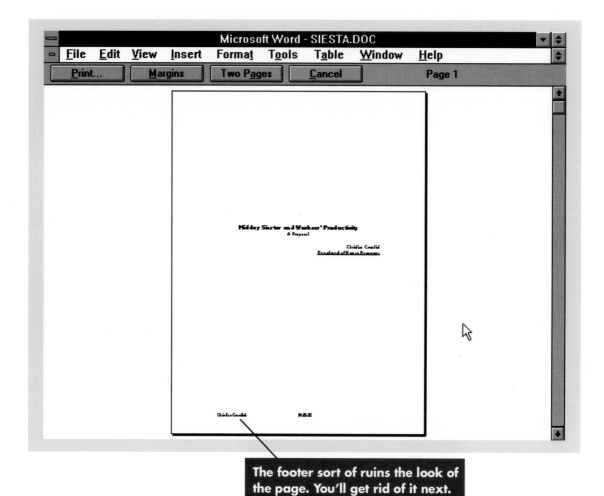

The footer sort of ruins the look of
the page. You'll get rid of it next.

If you want, use **PageDown** to thumb through the rest of the pages.
When you are finished browsing, click the <u>C</u>ancel or <u>C</u>lose button.

Now you just have to get rid of that footer on the first page. You might
be able to guess how.

Removing Headers, Footers, and Page Numbers from a Title Page

Start off as if you are creating a header or footer.

1. Pull down the <u>V</u>iew menu and select <u>H</u>eader/Footer.

2. In the dialog box that appears, click Different First <u>P</u>age, as shown:

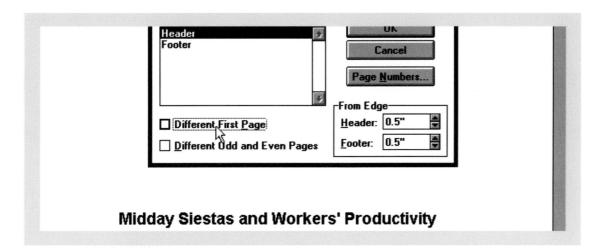

Midday Siestas and Workers' Productivity

If you actually wanted to make a separate header or footer for the first page, you could click First Header or First Footer and set one up. Since you want *no* footer on the first page, you're finished with this dialog box.

3. Click OK, as shown:

Quick Easy

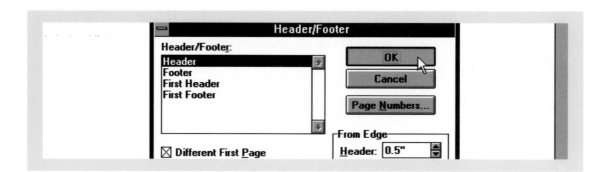

A header pane opens—a mere formality, I assure you.

● **Note** The pane opens because you clicked OK with Header highlighted in the Header/Footer dialog box. But you don't want to make a header, do you?

4. Click Close, as shown:

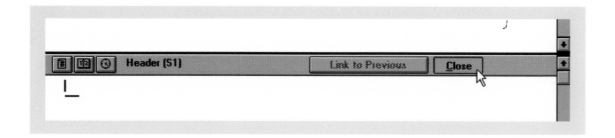

Now view the title page as a whole.

5. Pull down the <u>F</u>ile menu and select Print Pre<u>v</u>iew. Your screen should look like this:

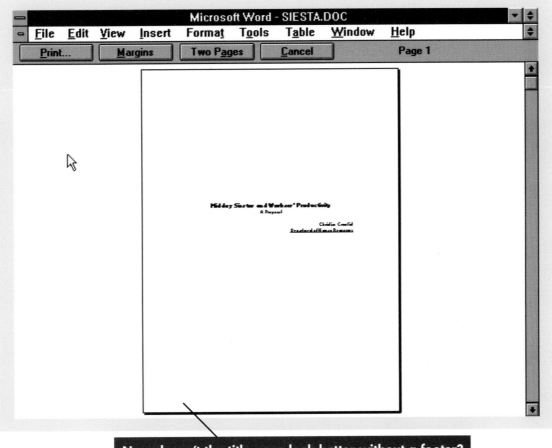

Now doesn't the title page look better without a footer?

6. Click <u>C</u>ancel.

7. Press Ctrl-Home.

That's it—a report ready for its audience. In the next and final part, I'll show you how to revise and improve your documents.

PART THREE

Revising Your Work

Although computers allow you to make instant changes and to edit easily as you go, it's still better to write a whole draft without the distraction of editing. Don't let the finished look of text on the screen sucker you into trying to perfect it or second-guessing yourself as you write. It's better to make editing a separate task. Come back later, print out your document, look it over, and *then* make your changes.

In this part I'll show you more than simple retyping. You'll see how to undo mistakes, copy and move text, make wholesale changes, and check your spelling.

Making Simple Changes and Corrections

19

Most of the editing you do to a document will be simple corrections. You print out the document, read it over, and mark your typos and the minor changes you want to make. Then you return to Word and touch up your document here and there. In this lesson I'll show you the basic set of editing techniques that you'll find yourself using most of the time.

Typing New Text Over Old

Usually, if you position the insertion point and begin typing, the words to the right of the insertion point are pushed along ahead of the words you are typing. This is called inserting text. It is possible to switch from Insert mode to what Word calls Overtype mode (although the rest of the world calls it Typeover). Then, when you position the insertion point and start typing, the letters you type replace the letters already there ("typing over" them). As you might imagine, this can be dangerous, but it's useful when you want to make a simple change. Let me show you an example. Start at the top of your SIESTA report.

1. Press **PageDown**.

2. Put the insertion point just before the letter *t* in the word *this,* on the third line of the first paragraph, as shown:

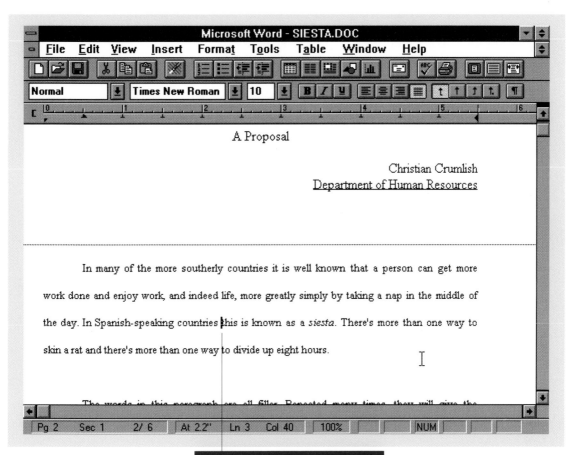

Put the insertion point here.

3. Press Insert (to the right of Backspace on most keyboards). OVR appears to the right of NUM at the bottom of the screen.

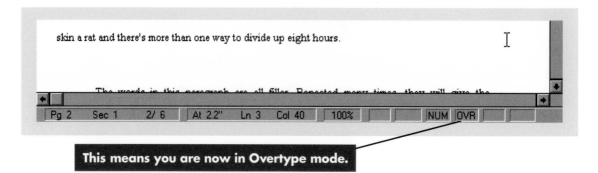

This means you are now in Overtype mode.

4. Type **people call this** and watch as the new words replace the old.

> work done and enjoy work, and indeed life, more greatly simply by taking a nap in the middle of
>
> the day. In Spanish-speaking countries people call this a *siesta*. There's more than one way to
>
> skin a rat and there's more than one way to divide up eight hours.

5. Press Insert again. **OVR** disappears.

This last step is very important. You can easily wreak havoc with your document if you forget you are in Overtype mode.

● Note Use Overtype only if the new text you intend to type is shorter or the same length as the old text you are replacing. (In the example you just tried, the new text was the same length as the old.) If the new text is longer, you'll replace text you don't want to replace unless you press Insert as soon as you reach the end of the text you intend to replace. Then it's probably not worth the bother of switching out of Insert mode.

There is also a way of indicating *first* what text you want to change, and then replacing it. We'll try that next.

Selecting the Text You Mean to Replace

Another basic editing maneuver is to select the text you want to replace and then simply type the new text. As soon as you start typing, the selection disappears, essentially replaced by what you type. (This works in Insert mode, *not* in Overtype.)

● **Note** If you want to keep the text you are replacing and use it elsewhere in your document, you need to move it. I'll discuss moving text in Lesson 22.

Try it now.

1. Select **people call this**.

work done and enjoy work, and indeed life, more greatly simply by taking a nap in the middle of

the day. In Spanish-speaking countries people call this a *siesta*. There's more than one way to

skin a rat and there's more than one way to divide up eight hours.

2. Type **such a nap is called** and watch as the selection disappears and the new text is inserted.

work done and enjoy work, and indeed life, more greatly simply by taking a nap in the middle of

the day. In Spanish-speaking countries such a nap is called a *siesta*. There's more than one way

to skin a rat and there's more than one way to divide up eight hours.

139

Easy, isn't it? This method also has its dangers. If you forget you have text selected and just start typing, you'll replace your selection by mistake. This is another good reason for saving your document from time to time. (In the next lesson, I'll show you how to undo *some* mistakes.)

Other times you will want to delete a large amount of text.

Deleting Entire Selections

You can delete as much as you want, one letter at a time, with **Backspace** or **Delete**, as discussed in Lesson 2. But if you have a lot to get rid of, those methods are tedious. Once again, selecting the text first is the trick. Here's an example.

1. Press **PageDown**.

2. Select several sentences, beginning with *Of course* and ending with *perfect!* (and the space immediately after it).

appearance of a full-length document. On and on the paragraph rambles, drifting further and further into random-sounding strings of words. Of course, it doesn't really have to say anything *at all*. As long as it looks like a typical paragraph, it will do. Another sentence or two and it will be long enough. Just one more and it will be perfect! There, that ought to do it.

The space after the exclamation point is also part of the selection. If you missed it, hold down Shift and press →.

● Note When you are deleting text, you have to pay attention to things like spaces and blank lines or they'll pile up on you.

3. Press **Delete**. The sentences disappear, and the paragraph closes up.

further into random-sounding strings of words. There, that ought to do it.

The words in this paragraph are all filler. Repeated many times, they will give the appearance of a full-length document. On and on the paragraph rambles, drifting further and

There's one more shortcut I'd like to show you.

Deleting a Word at a Time

You can also delete one word at a time. This is faster than going a letter at a time, but not so sweeping as deleting an entire selection at once.

1. Press **Ctrl-Delete**. The word *There* disappears.

appearance of a full-length document. On and on the paragraph rambles, drifting further and

further into random-sounding strings of words. that ought to do it.

The words in this paragraph are all filler. Repeated many times, they will give the

Notice that the comma that came directly after the word was not deleted with it.

For these purposes, Word treats commas and periods as separate words. Now delete the rest of the sentence a word at a time.

141

2. Press **Ctrl-Delete** seven times.

> appearance of a full-length document. On and on the paragraph rambles, drifting further and
>
> further into random-sounding strings of words.|
>
> The words in this paragraph are all filler. Repeated many times, they will give the

So **Ctrl-Delete** erases the word to the *right* of the insertion point. (Remember, **Delete** by itself erases the letter to the right of the insertion point.) By the same token, **Ctrl-Backspace** erases the word to the *left* of the insertion point (just as **Backspace** by itself deletes the letter to the left of the insertion point).

3. Press **Ctrl-←** (not **Ctrl-Backspace** yet) twice to move the insertion point two words to the left.

> appearance of a full-length document. On and on the paragraph rambles, drifting further and
>
> further into random-sounding strings of|words.
>
> The words in this paragraph are all filler. Repeated many times, they will give the

4. Now, press **Ctrl-Backspace** twice.

> appearance of a full-length document. On and on the paragraph rambles, drifting further and
>
> further into random-sounding|words.
>
> The words in this paragraph are all filler. Repeated many times, they will give the

So you see, it's all very simple and straightforward.

● Note If the insertion point is in the middle of a word when you press Ctrl-Delete, the rest of the word, from the insertion point to the end, will be erased. If you press Ctrl-Backspace in the same situation, the beginning of the word, up to the insertion point, will be erased.

Now put the insertion point back at the beginning of the document.

5. Press Ctrl-Home.

This handful of tricks should be enough for most editing. In the next lesson, I'll show you how to undo a mistake.

5 MINUTES

I Wish I Hadn't...

20

O ops! It's bound to happen eventually (if it hasn't already). By mistake, you delete the paragraph you just spent half an hour working on. What do you do? Fortunately, Word provides you with a way of recovering from most mistakes like this.

You can't take back something you just said, and you can't unring a bell, but you can undo many actions you take in Word. You can only undo the *most recent* action, so you have to think fast after you make a mistake. If you just keep pounding away at the keyboard, your error will be set in stone. Well, not entirely. This is another reason to save your work regularly. If you find yourself stuck with a real ugly mistake that you can't undo, you can go back to the last saved version of your document. In most cases, however, Undo will do the job.

The Dos and Don'ts of Undoing Your Mistakes

Actions you can undo include typing, deletions (probably the most important), and most menu commands. Let me show you a typical example. Start from your SIESTA report.

1. Press Ctrl-End.

2. Press Ctrl-↑ twice to get the entire final paragraph on the screen.

3. Select the final paragraph, as shown:

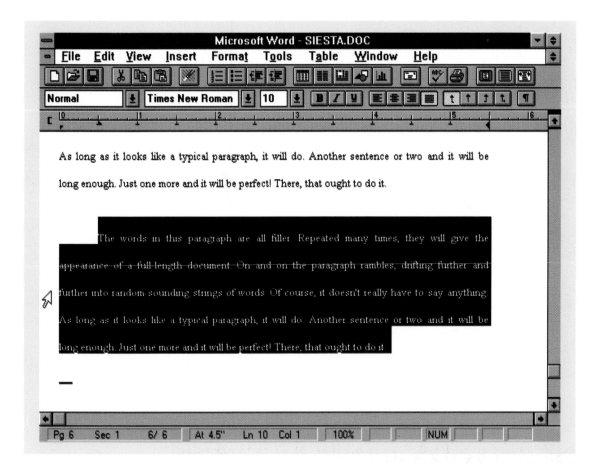

4. Now, "accidentally" press Delete. The paragraph disappears. Oh no!

long enough. Just one more and it will be perfect! There, that ought to do it.

Now you see it, now you don't.

But wait! All is not lost.

5. Pull down the <u>E</u>dit menu and select <u>U</u>ndo Edit Clear, as shown:

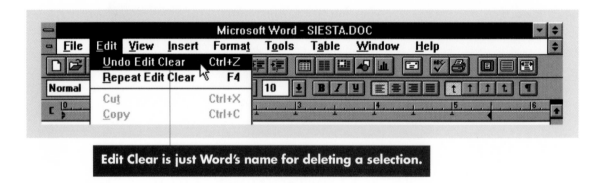

Edit Clear is just Word's name for deleting a selection.

The text reappears, intact—in fact, still selected.

● Note The exact wording of the Undo command varies depending on what action you just took.

There are things that you can't undo. For example, you can't undo a save. Here's what happens. (It's probably about time you saved anyway.)

6. Pull down the <u>F</u>ile menu and select <u>S</u>ave.

7. Now, pull down the <u>E</u>dit menu and look at the first option on the menu:

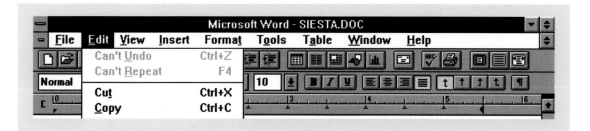

The menu option now reads Can't <u>U</u>ndo and it's "grayed out," which means the option is not currently available. Fortunately, Word *can* undo most of the things you'll want it to, as long as you act immediately.

Undo That Undo That You Do So Well

One of the things that you can undo is the Undo command itself. Why would you want to do this? Well, say you changed your mind, or realized that you actually *had* meant to do whatever you did. Here's an example:

1. If the last paragraph is no longer selected, select it again.

2. Press **Delete**, accidentally on purpose.

3. Pull down the <u>E</u>dit menu and select <u>U</u>ndo Edit Clear. (So far, you've done this all before.)

4. Now, pull down the <u>E</u>dit menu again, and select <u>U</u>ndo Undo, as shown:

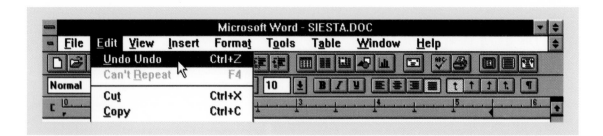

The paragraph is gone again. You can change your mind in this manner as many times as you like.

5. Pull down the <u>E</u>dit menu and select <u>U</u>ndo Edit Clear again.

Now it's back again.

If Worse Comes to Worst

If you screwed something up so bad that you'd give up your last half hour's work (or however much work you've done since you last saved) to fix it, there's something you can do even if you can't undo. It goes like this:

1. Pull down the <u>F</u>ile menu and select E<u>x</u>it.

2. When asked if you want to save changes to the document in which you made the mistake, click <u>N</u>o.

3. Save the changes to other documents you had open, if any.

4. Run Word again.

5. Open the document (it will be at the bottom of the <u>F</u>ile menu).

Do this only if the mistake is so bad that you can afford to lose whatever work you may have done since the last time you saved.

That's about all you need to know. In the upcoming lessons I'll be showing you other ways of editing your documents.

Easy Editing with Drag and Drop

21

In this lesson I'll show you a new feature of Word that really makes editing easier. It's called *drag and drop* and it allows you to click on a selection and drag it to a new location.

This is the way all word processors should work, because it allows you to grab letters, words, even whole sentences or paragraphs, and move them (or copy them) directly to a new location in your document. If you notice that you accidentally transposed two characters, you can drag one into place. You can move an introductory phrase to another part of the sentence. The possibilities are endless. I'll show you how to move text first and then how to copy.

Moving Text with Drag and Drop

Rearranging text is a common job in editing a document. Drag and drop is such an easy way to do it that it hardly needs an introduction. Try it now with the SIESTA report. Start at the top of the document.

1. Press **PageDown** twice (putting the middle of page 2 on the screen).

The insertion point is in the middle of the line because that's where it was at the top of the document.

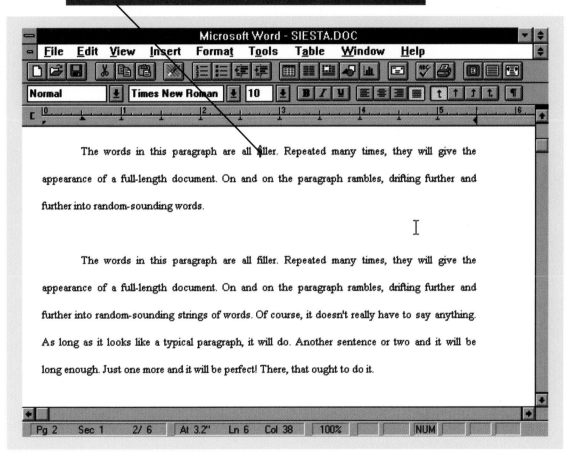

2. Select the second sentence in the first paragraph.

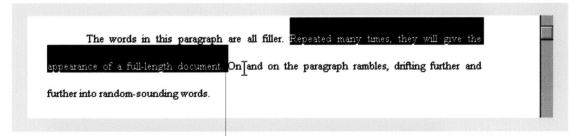

Make sure you include the space that comes at the end (you can hold down Ctrl and click anywhere in the sentence).

3. If it's not there already, move the mouse pointer to the selection (it will change from an insertion point to an arrow).

> The words in this paragraph are all filler. Repeated many times, they will give the appearance of a full-length document. On and on the paragraph rambles, drifting further and further into random-sounding words.

4. Click (and hold down) the mouse button. A gray box appears at the stem of the arrow, and a gray line appears near its point.

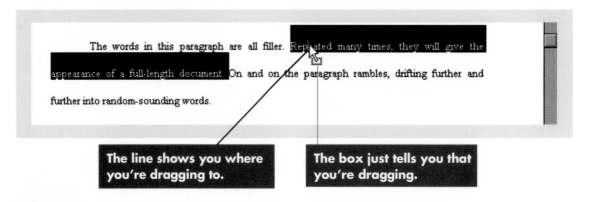

The line shows you where you're dragging to.

The box just tells you that you're dragging.

• Note You may find occasionally that you have started dragging a selection by mistake. This might happen when you've made a selection that's not exactly right, and you try selecting again in the same area. If you accidentally start inside the first selection, you'll be dragging it. Just release the mouse button, and then pull down the Edit menu and select Undo Move, if necessary.

5. While still holding down the mouse button, drag the pointer until the gray line is to the left of the *R* at the beginning of the second sentence in the next paragraph (the pointer will point directly to the *R*).

The words in this paragraph are all filler. Repeated many times, they will give the appearance of a full-length document. On and on the paragraph rambles, drifting further and further into random-sounding words.

The words in this paragraph are all filler. Repeated many times, they will give the

If you accidentally let go of the mouse button and lose your selection, just go back to step 2 and start over.

6. With the pointer in place, release the mouse button. The selection appears in the new location.

The words in this paragraph are all filler. On and on the paragraph rambles, drifting further and further into random-sounding words.

The words in this paragraph are all filler. Repeated many times, they will give the appearance of a full-length document. Repeated many times, they will give the appearance of a

Because the text you dropped into place is still selected, you can move it again using the same method if you are unhappy with its new position.

It's that easy.

• Note One drawback of drag and drop is that if you drag a selection past the bottom or top of the screen, the view scrolls very rapidly, making it difficult to drop the selection in a specific location more than one screen away from where you started. If this poses a problem for you, try the cut-and-paste approach described in the next lesson.

Copying Text with Drag and Drop

With drag and drop, you copy text almost exactly the same way as you move it. The difference is that you hold down Ctrl first. Try it.

1. Select *and on* (and the space after *on*) in the second paragraph.

appearance of a full-length document. Repeated many times, they will give the appearance of a

full-length document. On **and on** the paragraph rambles, drifting further and further into

random-sounding strings of words. Of course, it doesn't really have to say anything. As long as it

looks like a typical paragraph, it will do. Another sentence or two and it will be long enough. Just

If you don't get this space at the end of the selection, words will run together when you move it.

2. Point to the selection with the arrow.

3. Hold down Ctrl and drag the arrow until the gray line is just before the *t* in the word *the* that comes immediately after the selection.

appearance of a full-length document. Repeated many times, they will give the appearance of a full-length document. On ████ █████ the paragraph rambles, drifting further and further into random-sounding strings of words. Of course, it doesn't really have to say anything. As long as it looks like a typical paragraph, it will do. Another sentence or two and it will be long enough. Just

4. Release the mouse button and Ctrl. The selection is copied (and now the copy is selected).

appearance of a full-length document. Repeated many times, they will give the appearance of a full-length document. On and on ████ █████ the paragraph rambles, drifting further and further into random-sounding strings of words. Of course, it doesn't really have to say anything. As long as it looks like a typical paragraph, it will do. Another sentence or two and it will be long enough. Just

And that's all there is to drag and drop. (Now press Ctrl-Home to return to the top of the document.)

Rearranging Text with Cut, Copy, and Paste

22

In the previous lesson I mentioned one drawback of drag and drop: It is hard to control if you need to scroll to the destination. So when you need more control, there is another way to move and copy text. To move text, you cut it and then paste it elsewhere. If you copy and then paste, the original text is not moved.

Cut-and-Paste Editing

When you cut selected text, it is removed from the document but saved on something called the Clipboard. Then when you paste it, it is copied from the Clipboard to the new location.

Try it now with the memo you wrote in Part One.

1. Open the MEMO document (or switch to it if you already have it open).

2. Select the first sentence in the second paragraph.

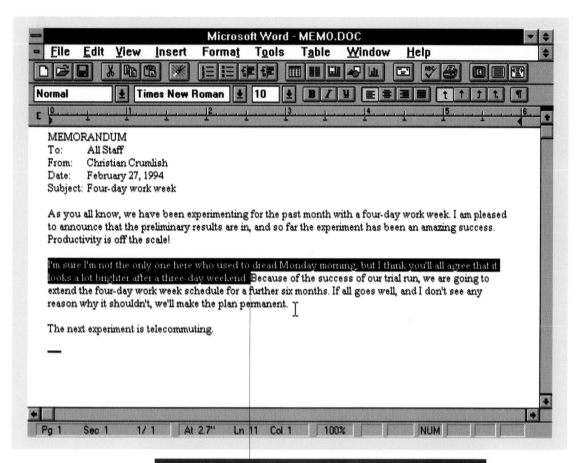

Again, it is important that your selection include this space after the sentence.

3. Pull down the Edit menu and select Cut, as shown:

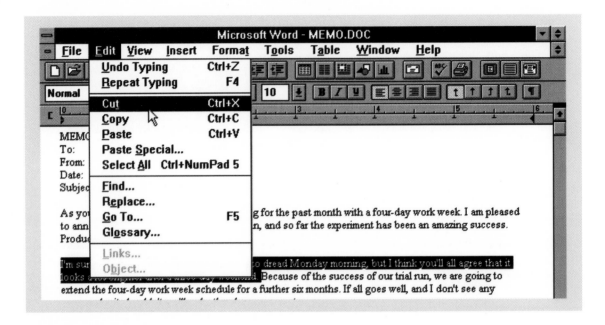

The text disappears:

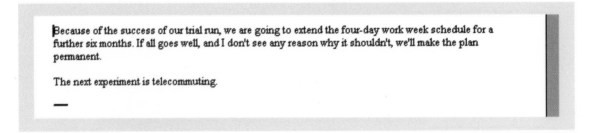

Don't worry, though. It's on the Clipboard I mentioned earlier.

4. Move the insertion point just to the left of the *I* in the word
If that begins the next sentence.

Because of the success of our trial run, we are going to extend the four-day work week schedule for a further six months. If all goes well, and I don't see any reason why it shouldn't, we'll make the plan permanent.

The next experiment is telecommuting.

5. Now pull down the Edit menu and select Paste, as shown:

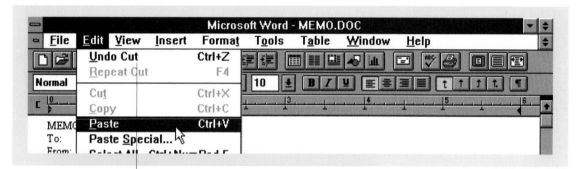

Notice here it says **Undo Cut**. You could still back out now if you wanted to.

The sentence is pasted in the new location.

Because of the success of our trial run, we are going to extend the four-day work week schedule for a further six months. I'm sure I'm not the only one here who used to dread Monday morning, but I think you'll all agree that it looks a lot brighter after a three-day weekend. If all goes well, and I don't see any reason why it shouldn't, we'll make the plan permanent.

The next experiment is telecommuting.

The sentence is also still on the Clipboard. (It will stay on the Clipboard until something new is copied or cut, or until you quit Windows.)

6. Pull down the <u>E</u>dit menu and select <u>P</u>aste (again). The sentence is pasted a second time.

Because of the success of our trial run, we are going to extend the four-day work week schedule for a further six months. I'm sure I'm not the only one here who used to dread Monday morning, but I think you'll all agree that it looks a lot brighter after a three-day weekend. I'm sure I'm not the only one here who used to dread Monday morning, but I think you'll all agree that it looks a lot brighter after a three-day weekend. If all goes well, and I don't see any reason why it shouldn't, we'll make the plan permanent.

The next experiment is telecommuting.

Here is the sentence once.   **And here it is again.**

The sentence will stay on the Clipboard until something else is put there or until you quit Windows, whichever comes first. You don't really want a second copy of that sentence, do you?

7. Pull down the <u>E</u>dit menu and select <u>U</u>ndo Paste.

Now I'll show you how to copy text (the procedure is very similar).

Copying (and Pasting)

When you cut and paste, the text is removed from its original location. The only difference when you copy and paste is that the text remains in its original location.

1. Select the short sentence at the end of the first paragraph.

As you all know, we have been experimenting for the past month with a four-day work week. I am pleased to announce that the preliminary results are in, and so far the experiment has been an amazing success. Productivity is off the scale!

Because of the success of our trial run, we are going to extend the four-day work week schedule for a further six months. I'm sure I'm not the only one here who used to dread Monday morning, but I think you'll all agree that it looks a lot brighter after a three-day weekend. If all goes well, and I don't see any reason why it shouldn't, we'll make the plan permanent.

There is no space at the end of this sentence because it's the last one in the paragraph.

2. Pull down the <u>E</u>dit menu and select <u>C</u>opy, as shown:

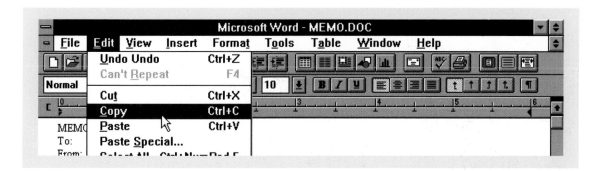

3. Now move the insertion point to the beginning of the last sentence in the memo.

Productivity is off the scale!

Because of the success of our trial run, we are going to extend the four-day work week schedule for a further six months. I'm sure I'm not the only one here who used to dread Monday morning, but I think you'll all agree that it looks a lot brighter after a three-day weekend. If all goes well, and I don't see any reason why it shouldn't, we'll make the plan permanent.

The next experiment is telecommuting.

4. Pull down the <u>E</u>dit menu and select <u>P</u>aste. The sentence is pasted in the new location.

Productivity is off the scale!

Because of the success of our trial run, we are going to extend the four-day work week schedule for a further six months. I'm sure I'm not the only one here who used to dread Monday morning, but I think you'll all agree that it looks a lot brighter after a three-day weekend. If all goes well, and I don't see any reason why it shouldn't, we'll make the plan permanent.

Productivity is off the scale!The next experiment is telecommuting.

The sentences run together because there was no space after the sentence you copied.

5. Type a space.

6. Press Home.

7. Press Delete.

8. Type **I'll say it again, p** (to provide an introductory phrase).

---

you'll all agree that it looks a lot brighter after a three-day weekend. If all goes well, and I don't see any reason why it shouldn't, we'll make the plan permanent.

I'll say it again, productivity is off the scale! The next experiment is telecommuting.

As with cutting, the sentence is still on the Clipboard and could be pasted in anywhere repeatedly. There is one other use for cut, copy, and paste worth knowing.

Copying from One Document to Another

You may sometimes be able to save yourself some work by copying a sentence or paragraph to a different document, even if you need to edit it slightly. It's almost as easy to do this as it is to copy within a document.

1. In your memo, select from the word *we* to the end of the first sentence of the first paragraph (as usual, include the space that comes after the sentence in your selection).

Date: February 27, 1994
Subject: Four-day work week

As you all know, we have been experimenting for the past month with a four-day work week. I am pleased to announce that the preliminary results are in, and so far the experiment has been an amazing success. Productivity is off the scale!

Because of the success of our trial run, we are going to extend the four-day work week schedule for a

2. Pull down the Edit menu and select Copy.

3. Pull down the Window menu and select **SIESTA.DOC** (or open it if it's no longer open).

4. Put the insertion point just before the first word of the first sentence of the second paragraph. (From the top, hit Page-Down twice, then ↑, and then Home twice.)

5. Pull down the <u>E</u>dit menu and select <u>P</u>aste. The text from the memo appears.

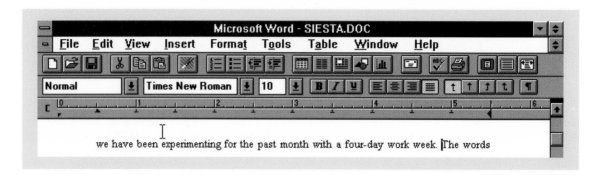

6. Press Home.

7. Press Delete.

8. Type **W**.

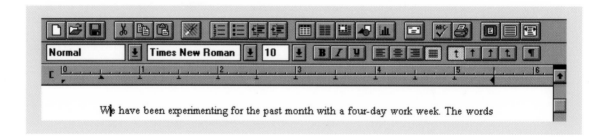

So that's how you copy from one document to another. You can do the same thing with cut and paste as well. Save all the changes you've made to MEMO and SIESTA.

In the next lesson I'll show you how to search for specific words in your documents and how to change them automatically.

23

Finding Words and Replacing Them

If you're looking for a specific word or phrase in your document (say, a sentence you wanted to reread and possibly change), Word can help you find it. If you want to substitute a better word for one somewhere in your document, Word can replace it for you. In this lesson, I'll show you how to find words and how to replace the words you find. (Replacing is more fun.)

Seek and Ye Shall Find

If you don't have SIESTA open, open it. And if you're not at the top of the document, press Ctrl-Home to get there.

Finding a specific word in a document is easy. Take, for example, the word *experimenting*. In the previous lesson, you copied a phrase that included that word. What if you don't remember where you put it, exactly? No problem. Just follow these steps:

1. Pull down the Edit menu and select Find, as shown:

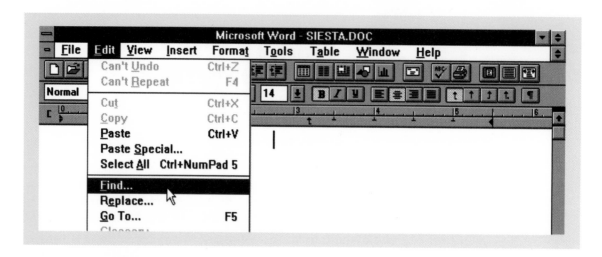

You'll see this dialog box:

Down means "from the insertion point down"—in other words, search the document forward. Up means search the part of the document above the insertion point. It doesn't matter much which direction you search in unless your document is extremely long, because when Word reaches the end (or beginning) of your document, it can go back to the beginning (or end) and keep searching.

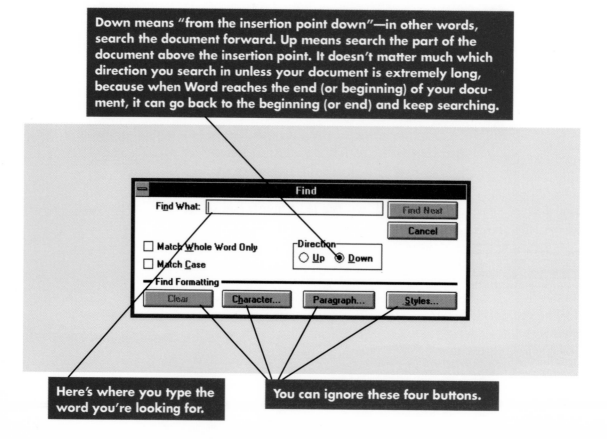

Here's where you type the word you're looking for.

You can ignore these four buttons.

Was the word *experiment* or *experimenting*? If you don't remember, it's safe to search for the shorter word (since it's also part of the longer one).

2. Type **experiment**. (Don't type the period.)

• Note If you hit ↵ after typing your word, it has the same effect as clicking OK (or in this case, Find Next). That may work out just fine, but you should develop the habit of *not* just hitting ↵ when typing in a dialog box because sometimes you'll have other things to do before clicking OK. (In this case, though, there is nothing else to do first.)

3. Click Find Next. Word finds *experiment* and highlights it.

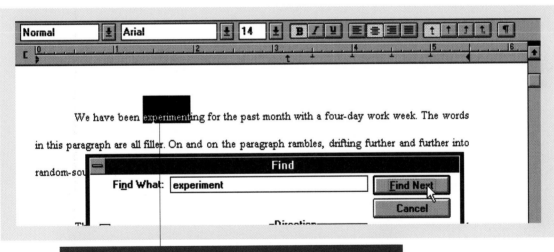

It was *experimenting* after all, but Word found it anyway. Notice that only part of the word is highlighted.

That's how you find words. When you are finished finding things, you've got to get out of this dialog box.

4. Click Cancel.

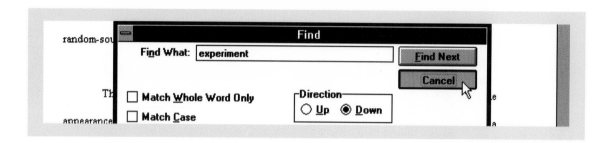

The word you found stays highlighted until you select something else. Be careful not to erase your selection by mistake.

Replacing One Word with Another

But wait. There's more. Word also gives you the ability to replace one word with another. It can be a smooth way to edit. Don't like that word? Replace it!

The next paragraph in SIESTA mentions "strings of words." Maybe "streams of words" would sound better.

● Note Replace works just like Find. (Think of Replace as "Find and Replace.") Everything you've learned about Find so far applies to Replace.

1. If your last selection is still highlighted, press ←.

● Note You don't need to know why you just did that, but if you don't do it, it messes up the replacing. Trust me on this.

2. Pull down the Edit menu and select Replace, as shown:

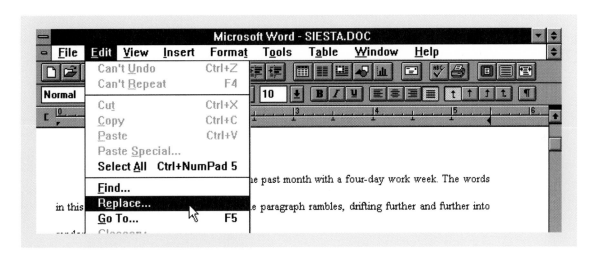

This dialog box appears:

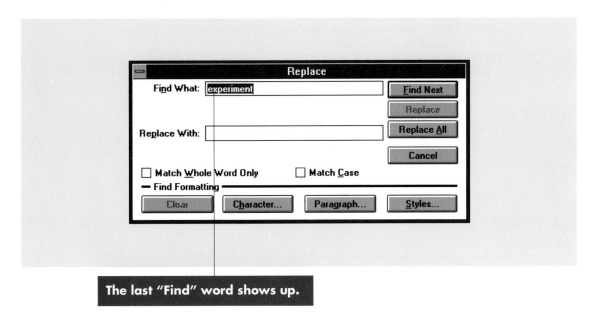

The last "Find" word shows up.

3. Type **string** in the Find What text box (*don't* press ↵).

4. Press Tab.

5. Type **stream** in the Replace With text box.

6. Click Find Next.

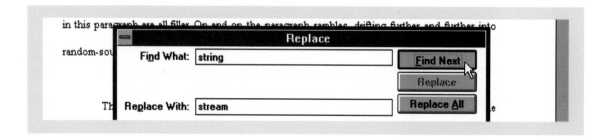

Found!

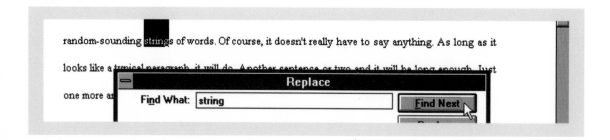

Now, the moment we've all been waiting for.

7. Click Replace.

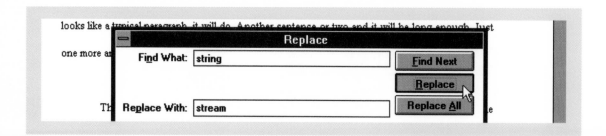

It's done. I know it appears as though nothing has happened. The word *string* is still highlighted. But you're looking at the next paragraph. (The scroll box is a little lower on the right.) You see, choosing the Replace button replaces the word *and* moves you to the next occurrence of the word (like Find Next). That's so you can make the same replacement over and over. But let's make sure *stream* really did replace *string*.

8. Click Close.

9. Press PageUp.

See, it did change.

appearance of a full-length document. On and on the paragraph rambles, drifting further and

further into random-sounding streams of words. Of course, it doesn't really have to say anything.

As long as it looks like a typical paragraph, it will do. Another sentence or two and it will be

long enough. Just one more and it will be perfect! There, that ought to do it.

The word is now *streams*.

That's all you really need to know about Find and Replace.

10 MINUTES

Fixing Spelling Mistakes

24

My sister used to say that when she grew up she would have a secretary who would check all her spelling. Word provides you with the next best thing—a spell-checker. Word compares your spellings with its internal dictionary. When you're trying to write, you shouldn't have to worry about spelling or typos. Write freely, and then go back and check.

Grist for the Mill

First, to give the spelling checker a workout, you'll need to enter a sample paragraph.

1. Start a new document.

> **● Note** If you need a refresher, Lesson 7 explains how to start a new document.

2. Type the following paragraph, warts and all:

Job-related stress can sometimes be aleviated by by doing a simple stretching excercise or by saying a nonsense word, such as "mang." It is good to stand up and leave your desk even if you do not plan to excercise, according to Dr. Grieble. THe point is to interrupt your routine. ⏎

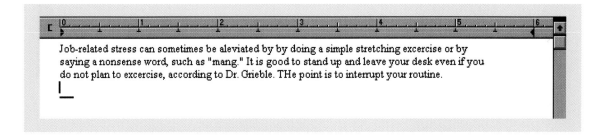

Job-related stress can sometimes be aleviated by by doing a simple stretching excercise or by saying a nonsense word, such as "mang." It is good to stand up and leave your desk even if you do not plan to excercise, according to Dr. Grieble. THe point is to interrupt your routine.

There are an abundance of errors in this poor paragraph. Let's see how many Word can catch.

No More I before E

Okay, maybe you can't afford to forget all the spelling rules you ever learned, but you can count on Word to find glaring errors.

You can start a spelling check from anywhere in your document. When Word reaches the end, it will ask you whether it should continue from the start. But you might as well begin at the beginning.

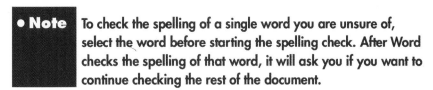

• Note To check the spelling of a single word you are unsure of, select the word before starting the spelling check. After Word checks the spelling of that word, it will ask you if you want to continue checking the rest of the document.

1. Press Ctrl-Home.

2. Click the Spelling button on the Toolbar (the one with the tiny ABC), as shown:

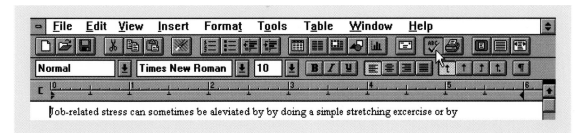

This dialog box appears:

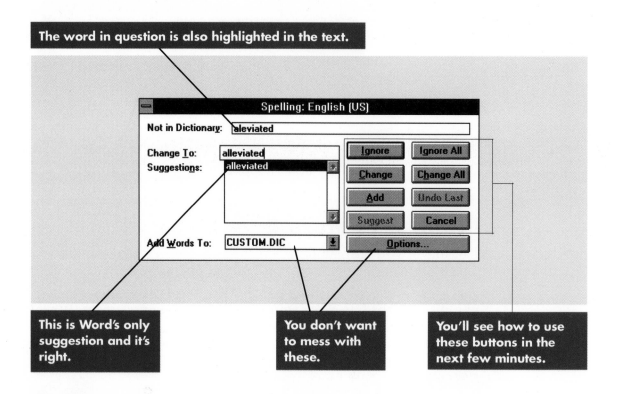

The word in question is also highlighted in the text.

This is Word's only suggestion and it's right.

You don't want to mess with these.

You'll see how to use these buttons in the next few minutes.

● **Note** You can quit a spelling check at any time by clicking Cancel
or Close.

Oh, right, *alleviate*. When Word's suggestion is correct, as it is now,
you tell it to make the change.

3. Click Change.

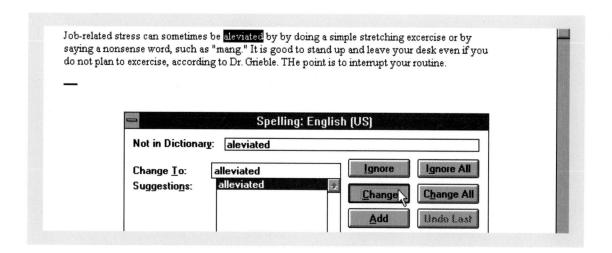

Job-related stress can sometimes be aleviated by by doing a simple stretching excercise or by saying a nonsense word, such as "mang." It is good to stand up and leave your desk even if you do not plan to excercise, according to Dr. Grieble. THe point is to interrupt your routine.

Spelling: English (US)

Not in Dictionary: aleviated

Change To: alleviated
Suggestions: alleviated

Ignore   Ignore All
Change   Change All
Add   Undo Last

Another word is questioned. In this case, the problem is the *by by*. The dialog box changes slightly for this situation.

4. Click Delete.

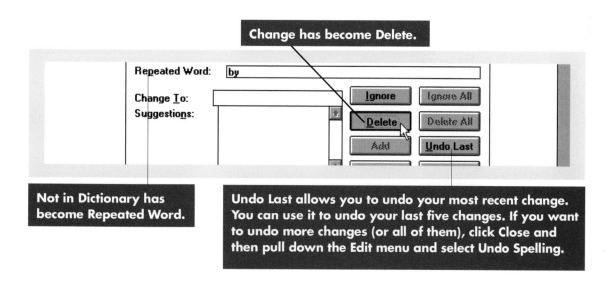

Change has become Delete.

Repeated Word: by

Change To:
Suggestions:

Ignore   Ignore All
Delete   Delete All
Add   Undo Last

Not in Dictionary has become Repeated Word.

Undo Last allows you to undo your most recent change. You can use it to undo your last five changes. If you want to undo more changes (or all of them), click Close and then pull down the Edit menu and select Undo Spelling.

Quick Easy

The spelling *excercise* is incorrect. Because it's an error that appears in more than one place, you should take care of both cases at once. (Imagine if you had misspelled a word throughout a 50-page report!)

5. Click Change All.

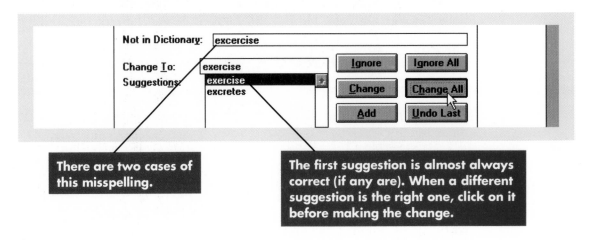

There are two cases of this misspelling.

The first suggestion is almost always correct (if any are). When a different suggestion is the right one, click on it before making the change.

Word can't find *mang* in the dictionary, which is reassuring. Tell Word to ignore this one.

6. Click Ignore.

saying a nonsense word, such as "mang." It is good to stand up and leave your desk even if you do not plan to excercise, according to Dr. Grieble. THe point is to interrupt your routine.

Spelling: English (US)

Not in Dictionary: mang

Change To: magna

Suggestions:
magna
mange
mango
man
manage
mangy

Ignore	Ignore All
Change	Change All
Add	Undo Last
Suggest	Close

Note Don't be concerned if you notice that the second *excercise* has not been corrected yet. It will happen automatically when Word gets to it.

Grieble could not be found in the dictionary. You'll probably use his name again if you used it once, so add it to the dictionary or you'll have to ignore it over and over in the future.

7. Click Add.

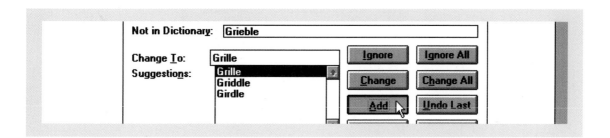

Another kind of typo is discovered—the kind where you don't let up on Shift in time.

8. Click Change again.

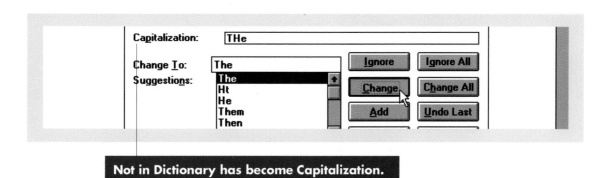

Not in Dictionary has become Capitalization.

A dialog box appears to tell you that the spelling check is finished.

9. Click OK. (What else could you do?)

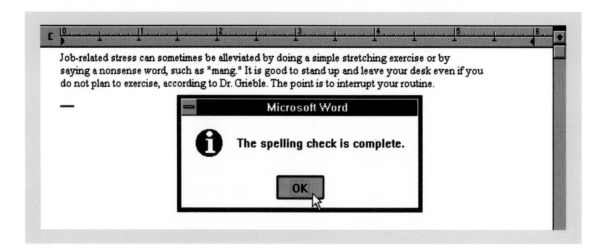

Word will not always find every spelling error in a document. For instance, some misspelled words are just different words spelled correctly. Word will never catch it if you use *their* when you mean *they're*, for instance, so don't rely on the spell-checker completely. Keep a dictionary handy.

Well, you're done with this book! You can now write, format, and edit documents in Word. Congratulations.

Where Do I Go from Here?

In this short amount of time, you've learned most of the things you'll ever need to know about Word for Windows. Even the most advanced users of the program spend most of their time doing the things you've learned from this book. Still, you might reach a point where you want to know a little more about Word's other capabilities. For example, you might want to learn how to use some of Word's advanced printing features, such as printing envelopes; or how to make lists automatically; or how to set up tables or columns to organize information; or how to draw simple shapes or produce charts and graphs; or how to use Word's grammar checker in addition to the spelling checker; or how to find better words in the Thesaurus.

If you'd like to stick with a beginner's approach, learning in short, easy lessons and trying things out step-by-step, then **ABC's of Microsoft Word for Windows, Version 2.0**, Alan R. Neibauer, SYBEX, 1992, is the right book for you. It covers the material in this book with a little more explanation, and then continues on and explains some of the more useful advanced features.

If you think you're ready for a how-to book that doubles as a reference and covers Word in depth, try **Mastering Microsoft Word for Windows, Version 2.0**, Michael J. Young, SYBEX, 1992. It's full of great examples and hands-on steps, and it explains everything from the most basic topics to the most advanced.

If you'd like a quick reference book to answer occasional questions, then you want **Microsoft Word for Windows, Version 2.0 Instant Reference**, Robert Shepherd, SYBEX, 1992.

INDEX

●

 ● Note Page numbers in purple are found in Part One.
Page numbers in blue are found in Part Two.
Page numbers in green are found in Part Three.

Symbols

[(bracket symbol) on ruler, 110–111

↵ (Enter) key, 9

A

alignment, options on ribbon, 81–82

Arrange All (Window menu), 47

Auto Spacing, 95

automatic save, 21–23

B

Backspace, 10–13

beginning of document, moving insertion point to, 54

Bold button (ribbon), 71–72

boldface text, 71–72

bottom of document, moving to, 56

bottom margin, 104

bracket symbol ([) on ruler, 110–111

C

cables for printers, 28–31

Cancel button, 26, 34

capitalization, spelling check of, 177

Center Alignment button (ribbon), 81

centering text on page, 129

Clipboard, 156, 158, 160

Copy option (Edit menu), 161, 163

Copy button (Toolbar), 51–52

copying, 160–163

documents, 163–164